Difficult Conversations in Education, Health and Social Care

This accessible guide combines evidence-based research with practical experience to help develop effective communication skills for navigating difficult or challenging situations.

The book delves into what it means to be an effective and confident communicator, before addressing how to approach those often-avoided 'difficult conversations.' Key features include:

- Strategies for tackling tough topics, from handling emotional outbursts to addressing both conscious and unconscious reactions
- Approaches for discussing sensitive issues like trauma, sexuality, gender, race, and serious concerns
- Engaging case studies, scenarios, activities, and top tips to support discussions
- Practical advice on how to enhance communication skills and prevent difficult conversations from escalating
- Exploring concepts and techniques that can be applied across various professions and in personal life

The authors emphasise the importance of applying the right skills, knowledge, and experience to transform a challenging conversation into an effective, solution-focused, and collaborative exchange. With innovative ideas for making tough discussions more manageable, this book is an invaluable resource for professionals in education, social services, healthcare, and similar fields.

Becky Edwards is a Senior Lecturer in Childhood Studies at the University of Chichester, UK, an award-winning children's author and co-founder of the Parent and Carers Support Organisation (PACSO). In her roles as a primary school teacher, children's centre manager, and lecturer, Becky has extensive experience of supporting children, students, and families from diverse backgrounds in many different situations.

Chris Smethurst is Co-Director of the Institute of Education, Health, and Social Sciences at the University of Chichester, UK. Chris has a background in community work, youth work, residential childcare, and field social work, specialising in learning disabilities and mental health teams. Together with Becky, Chris co-developed the 'From Adversity to University' project, which helps marginalised individuals engage with higher education.

Difficult Conversations in Education, Health and Social Care

How to Talk About What Really Matters and What to Do When it All Goes Wrong

Becky Edwards and Chris Smethurst

Routledge
Taylor & Francis Group

LONDON AND NEW YORK

Designed cover image: © Tiana Leakey

First published 2025
by Routledge
4 Park Square, Milton Park, Abingdon, Oxon OX14 4RN

and by Routledge
605 Third Avenue, New York, NY 10158

Routledge is an imprint of the Taylor & Francis Group, an informa business

© 2025 Becky Edwards and Chris Smethurst

British Library Cataloguing-in-Publication Data
A catalogue record for this book is available from the British Library

Library of Congress Cataloging-in-Publication Data
Names: Edwards, Becky author | Smethurst, Christopher author
Title: Difficult conversations in education, health and social care : how to talk about what really matters and what to do when it all goes wrong / Becky Edwards and Chris Smethurst.
Description: Abingdon, Oxon ; New York, NY : Routledge, 2025. | Includes bibliographical references and index. |
Identifiers: LCCN 2024058075 (print) | LCCN 2024058076 (ebook) | ISBN 9781032559858 hardback | ISBN 9781032559841 paperback | ISBN 9781003433248 ebook
Subjects: LCSH: Communication in human services | Communication in education | Conflict management
Classification: LCC HV29.7 .E39 2025 (print) | LCC HV29.7 (ebook) | DDC 361.301/4—dc23/eng/20250318
LC record available at https://lccn.loc.gov/2024058075
LC ebook record available at https://lccn.loc.gov/2024058076

ISBN: 978-1-032-55985-8 (hbk)
ISBN: 978-1-032-55984-1 (pbk)
ISBN: 978-1-003-43324-8 (ebk)

DOI: 10.4324/9781003433248

Typeset in Optima
by codeMantra

For: Phoebe, Tiana, Marko, Juliette (and mum!)

To Ninesh, Mia and Joss.. Thank you for a lifetime of conversations..

Contents

1
Introduction
It's not just about words

What we are trying to do in this book

When we sat down to compile this book, we started from what we did *not* want to achieve. Our top priority was that we wanted to produce something that was *useful*. Having worked as both practitioners and academics, we understand the difficulty of translating what we read into something that we can apply in practice. There are many reasons for this. Firstly, we are both voracious readers, consuming vast quantities of text and words of wisdom – only to forget them within days. (If we are being honest, this is usually within minutes.) Secondly, we were struck that many 'how to' books, particularly in the categories of 'self-help' or management, seem to be reduced to simplistic lists of steps to take or life-affirming slogans. It is almost as if the complexities of human behaviour can be reduced to the start-up instructions for a mobile phone. And, anyway, if life were as simple as finding the '5 steps to happiness' or the '6 things you must do to find the person of your dreams', surely everyone would be doing it and the market for these books would dry up. We do add a caveat to this: we do both like the *7 Habits of Highly Effective People* by Steven Covey. Of course, we do not practise any of them, but it is a very useful and interesting volume. Whilst compiling this book, we discovered an 8th habit that we hope that Covey may be persuaded to add in a later addition: the eating of large quantities of crisps whilst striving to be effective authors. Any current or recent students will understand this approach to completing assignments (although you may wish to substitute coffee, chocolate or the energy drink of your choice for crisps). However, we will leave it to you, the reader, to judge whether this has made us effective authors, or not; so, let us explain our approach.

The title of this introductory chapter, 'It's not just about words', reflects three principles. Firstly, we know that communication is not just verbal; we may think that our well-crafted sentence will have our listeners spellbound.

DOI: 10.4324/9781003433248-1

It may bring us down to earth to learn that research reveals what they are really paying attention to: actual words – 7%; the way words are delivered (for example, tone, or emphasis on certain words) – 38%; facial expression – 55% (Moss, 2017). The obvious conclusion is that we could probably talk absolute rubbish as long as we look and sound convincing. Students of politics will not find this at all surprising. But, in our professions we do need to ensure that we are able to *communicate* content that is important, potentially life-changing or life-saving. Therefore, it is a good idea to understand what may improve or inhibit understanding of what we say and what others say to us.

Secondly, communication, particularly in difficult situations, is affected by context. For example, knowing what not to say or when to say nothing at all is as equally important as having verbal fluency. We are sure that we have all been in situations where well-meaning and wise people have been trying to assist or advise us; and we are very appreciative and know they are trying to help, but really wish that they would just shut up for a minute and leave us alone. Being able to read situations, to be empathic, and weigh up and time our interventions accordingly are key abilities in being able to have effective, difficult conversations. Patterson et al. (2002) conducted research which indicated that having these abilities was both highly prized in organisations and respected by colleagues. We will return to this study at various points in the book. The research conducted by Patterson et al. added to what others had written about the importance of capabilities such as *emotional intelligence* (Mayer et al., 2011; Goleman, 2020). Integral to these concepts is the possession of self-knowledge, which is why it is imperative to understand that, when having difficult conversations, we also come with our own pre-conceptions, histories, strengths and weaknesses. These may enable or hinder us according to context, our mood, and even the time of day. Consequently, our book contains theoretical knowledge, which we hope will be useful in developing understanding of ourselves and others. This brings us to the final element of our approach.

We started writing with the intention of addressing our own experience of frequent struggles to apply detailed theories, methods and techniques in the real world. This can be particularly problematic, where situations are complex and rapidly changing. In short, we can learn much about the theory of driving a car from a book, but may struggle to apply this consistently, if at all, when on the open road. In the field of communication, theories may not appear to 'fit', or we may struggle to be sufficiently mentally agile, particularly if emotions are high. Therefore, this book, and the chapters within it, does not comprise an instruction manual; instead, we hope that you will find some useful nuggets of information that you can apply in your own lives. You will not remember all of the content; but particularly if you have spent your well-earned money, we hope that your reading experience will be punctuated by exclamations of "I never knew that!" and "Oh, that's why that happens!" and not "I wish I'd saved my money!"

We would ask that you do not skim-read each chapter in the hope that there will be a top tips section that bypasses the boring bits. Nevertheless, each chapter will conclude with a 'key takeaways' section. We sincerely believe that each chapter is worth reading, and we will summarise the content below. But, before we do that, it is probably worth us starting with what we mean by 'difficult conversations'.

We understand that what constitutes a difficult conversation for one person may not be so for another. Similarly, the topic or focus of the discussion, in itself, may not be difficult, but the timing of it may be. Or parties may enter a discussion in an emotional context that is fraught or characterised by presupposition, suspicion and the 'fear of losing'. Consequently, for the purposes of this book, we have kept our definition of 'difficult conversations' very broad. As a working definition we feel that the model of *crucial* conversations by Patterson et al. (2002) has much to recommend it. Their definition featured three key elements:

- Opposing opinions
- Strong emotions
- High stakes

Of course, difficult conversations do not just refer to ones that are potentially conflictual; they may involve situations where we do not know what to say or are afraid of saying the wrong thing. This can lead to us avoiding difficult conversations, being embarrassed, or being over-critical of ourselves when we think we have made a mess of things (Chrisler, 2008; Alcolado & Radomsky, 2011; Kelly-Turner & Radomsky, 2022). Therefore, the chapters will provide useful information on topics where people often worry that they will say the wrong thing, cause offence, or believe that they had better not say anything and leave well alone. Unfortunately, the book does not have the scope or word count to cover all the topics that would be useful inclusions; there are inevitable omissions, some of them significant. However, when compiling a book of this nature, deciding what to leave out is as complicated as identifying what should be included. Therefore, where there are potential omissions, these are generally topics that we feel have been covered extensively in other volumes. Let us turn now to a brief summary of what is included in each chapter.

The book in detail

In addition to the Introduction and Conclusion, we have divided the book into three parts:

- How to have effective conversations
- Why does it all go wrong – again and again... and again?
- How to talk about what really matters

'How to have effective conversations' is a 'getting started' part, containing three chapters. The first chapter in this part, 'Being an effective communicator', introduces us to some of the key, underpinning principles of successful communication. It explores the theme returned to throughout the book, that communication is far more than merely spoken words. You may already be familiar with many of the theories and principles, but the chapter provides a firm foundation for what follows in the book, not least the second chapter, 'Are you really listening?' This chapter explores the difference between hearing and listening and discusses the important characteristics of what it takes to be a good listener. The final chapter in this part takes the learning from the previous two chapters and applies it to difficult conversations. In 'How to take the "difficult" out of difficult conversations', we will explore the preparatory thinking and understanding that enables us to have effective discussions. When writing this book, we both shared accounts of the times when we were surprised that our good intentions were misinterpreted by others – and that, in retrospect, the disaster that followed might have been obvious to anyone who had stopped to think things through. Therefore, this chapter has been written with the intention of enabling us to predict and address the things that undermine our best efforts to be skilful communicators.

The chapter 'How to take the "difficult" out of difficult conversations' provides a bridge into the next part of the book where we will explore 'Why does it all go wrong – again and again... and again? If the first part of the book focuses on preparatory work for difficult conversations, this part is primarily concerned with how to take remedial action when things go wrong. In addition, we discuss why we and others may unwittingly repeat the same destructive patterns in our communication, why we say things we may later regret and lose sight of the things we want to achieve. The first chapter, 'Monkeys with smartphones? When our emotions take control', demonstrates how the brain's processes, which are designed to keep us safe, can unconsciously lead us and the people we are communicating with to be defensive or adversarial. We will explore why our ability to communicate can desert us when we are under stress, why we may become inarticulate, forgetful, and/or experience 'brain fog' just when we need to be at our sharpest.

'It's all about relationships' explores some of the psychological processes discussed in the previous chapter and applies them in the wider context of our ability to engage with others. This is particularly important when we are trying to convince someone of our good intentions or invite them to consider their viewpoint from a different perspective. Consequently, we discuss why it is that people do not change their minds and, in fact, can take up even more entrenched positions when we confront them with information that challenges their views. We will also consider why people often like to feel 'hard done-by' and how they can, often unconsciously, manipulate conversations so that they feel aggrieved.

The final chapter of this part, '"Charlie is having a bad day!" A case study', brings together the themes discussed in the preceding chapters and applies them in the context of a fictional case study. It offers some reflections and suggestions about managing email conversations and introduces some approaches to conducting negotiations.

The final part of the book, 'How to talk about what really matters', explores specific themes in relation to race, sexuality, gender, and trauma. However, the first chapter, 'Communication in context', provides an overview of the influence of organisational and professional cultures on the way practitioners communicate and are expected to communicate. It considers the influence of these cultures in creating the conditions for poor communication and how this can lead to catastrophic consequences. Critically, it discusses the impact of working under conditions of high pressure, uncertainty, and with an underpinning fear of blame.

In 'How to talk about sexuality and gender', Rylee Spooner addresses the reality that many people may be worried about saying the wrong thing, unwittingly giving offence and perhaps being unsure about terminology. Consequently, the chapter begins with 'A whistlestop tour of language' before addressing key themes such as 'Conversations around coming out' and 'How to bring up identity'. Underpinned by wry humour, Rylee's chapter is both a refreshing and challenging exploration of key issues.

Mia Edwards' chapter, 'Uncomfortable conversations about race', provides a powerful rebuttal to those who refuse to engage with the realities of overt and insidious racism. The chapter uses personal experience and astute political analysis to provide tools and techniques for whom Mia terms, 'the exhausted and for the invigorated; for the enraged and the curious'.

In the chapter 'Trauma-informed approaches', Sam McNally draws upon extensive experience both as a teacher and nurse to explore the impact of trauma on the individual's perception of the world and their response to it. With a specific focus on education and health settings, Sam demonstrates how our understanding of trauma can and should enhance our professional and personal communication.

Conclusion

We hope that you will read the chapters in sequence; we have structured the book so that each part and every chapter within each part builds on the previous one. However, chapters can be read in isolation, so the reader can dip in and out of the book's content as they see fit. In most chapters we have included case studies to illustrate key themes, but our intention has been to write the content in such a way that, we hope, makes sense and resonates with the reader's own experience and understanding.

References

Alcolado, G.M., & Radomsky, A.S. (2011). Believe in yourself: Manipulating beliefs about memory causes checking. *Behaviour Research and Therapy, 49*(1), 42–49.

Chrisler, J.C. (2008). 2007 Presidential address: Fear of losing control: Power, perfectionism, and the psychology of women. *Psychology of Women Quarterly, 32*(1), 1–12.

Goleman, D. (2020). *Emotional intelligence: Why it can matter more than IQ.* London: Bloomsbury Publishing.

Kelly-Turner, K., & Radomsky, A.S. (2022). Always saying the wrong thing: Negative beliefs about losing control cause symptoms of social anxiety. *Cognitive Therapy and Research, 46*(6), 1137–1149.

Mayer, J.D., Salovey, P., Caruso, D.R., & Cherkasskiy, L. (2011). *Emotional intelligence.* Cambridge: Cambridge University Press.

Moss, B. (2017). *Communication skills in health and social care.* London: Sage.

Patterson, K., Grenny, J., McMillan, R., & Switzler, A. (2002). *Crucial conversations: Tools for talking when stakes are high.* New York: McGraw-Hill Education.

Part 1

How to have effective conversations

2

How to be an effective communicator

Introduction

This chapter explores the different ways in which we communicate and why effective communication is so important in difficult conversations. It looks at the importance of body language, gesture and intonation in communication and conversation and how to ensure that our message is consistent and clear. There will always be situations where effective communication becomes more difficult. This chapter considers what to do when this happens and how to ensure that what we are saying is understood by those who are listening to us. It also considers the ways in which emails and texts can be easily misunderstood and how to remedy this. In difficult conversations, being an effective communicator becomes crucial. Let's begin by looking at why.

Why communication is important

As humans we are born communicating. The first sound we make is a cry for attention, an announcement to others that we have arrived. That initial cry reflects the essence of what it means to be a good communicator: the intrinsic ability to express a want, need or emotion and the extrinsic need for someone to respond to us; we 'cannot not communicate' (Rosengren, 2006: 38). Our innate desire to express our feelings, to explain what we need and who we want to fulfil that need, is crucial in shaping our understanding of who we are and where we fit in the world. If we communicate effectively and are responded to appropriately, the world feels safe and we feel valued. When this does not happen, when our voice is not heard and our needs are not met, the world becomes scary, uncertain, and unpredictable (Lindon, 2016).

DOI: 10.4324/9781003433248-3

When does communication become conversation?

This dependence on communication, the desire to make ourselves understood, our need to create and share information with others in order to reach a mutual understanding (Rogers, 1951), is an integral part of being human. As we grow, we try constantly to interactively align with others, not just to communicate but to engage with them, to have conversations. We are designed for dialogue rather than monologue (Garrod & Pickering, 2004), but the problem with dialogue, with conversation, is that it depends not only on *our* ability to communicate effectively but on the ability of others to communicate with us and, more importantly, on our capacity to understand each other. The cry that announces our arrival in the world is communication: 'I'm here', 'I'm cold', 'I'm scared', 'I'm hungry'. How we respond, how we initially interact by holding, hugging, comforting, making eye contact, talking – these are the seeds of conversation. Studies by Hall and Morella (2020) prove that affectionate interactions that show you care – a mother responding to a child, couples hugging each other, the support of friends – have both psychological and physiological benefits. Such supportive social interactions, these caring conversations, have been shown to reduce loneliness and depression (Morelli et al., 2014; Piferi & Lawler, 2006), decrease blood pressure and stress, enhance well-being, and reduce our risk of mortality. Effective communication and meaningful conversations can, quite literally, save our lives.

So how can we make sure that our conversations are always beneficial and life-enhancing? That outcomes are always positive rather than negative? That our conversations make everyone involved feel better, not worse? That we all leave the conversation feeling stronger, not weaker? Listened to, not silenced?

The truth is that we can't.

Conversations are complicated. They demand emotional understanding both of ourselves and of the others involved. Conversations demand self-awareness: what am I thinking and feeling? What am I hoping will happen? But also, am I aware of what others in the conversation are thinking and feeling and hoping will happen? They demand the ability to read body language and non-verbal cues and to understand that what is *not* said is often more important than what *is* said (Stone et al., 2021). And often we are trying to focus on all of this whilst in the middle of a busy hospital environment or a classroom full of children or in the home of a family who just want us to go away and leave them alone.

Conversations can be life-saving, but we also spend much of our lives dreading them. There is no guarantee that they will end positively or have the impact that we hope for; if there were such a guarantee, there would be no difficult conversations and no need for this book. But there are ideas and strategies that can help, tools that can be used to develop more effective communication. And they almost always start with building a trusting relationship.

To be 'professional', first be a human being

Case study: Jack

Jack is 2 years old and started experiencing pain when he was on holiday with his parents. As the day progressed the pain seemed to get worse, and Jack's distress increased. They took him to the nearest hospital but the staff there were unable to work out what the problem was and referred them to a bigger hospital with more specialised staff. The parents are overwrought, exhausted, and worried. They are not sure what is wrong with their son and are feeling isolated, far away from the family and friends who would usually support them. At the new hospital, Jack is examined by a surgeon. After the examination the surgeon asks to meet with Jack's parents.

The surgeon must explain to them that it appears that Jack has a testicular torsion, a twisted testicle, which needs emergency surgery and that there is the potential that the testicle will need to be removed.

What can the surgeon do or say?

In the scenario above, the surgeon has a limited amount of time to explain complicated procedures and discuss potentially life-changing options with the parents. How do we do this? How do we engender confidence and communicate clearly when stakes are high, emotions are strong, and time is limited (Patterson et al., 2002)?

'I sit down with them. I make them feel that we have time, that I will answer any questions they have', says the surgeon from this case study. 'It's about being genuine, about being open, honest and clear about using language

that everyone can understand rather than medical jargon. I always tell my patients that I don't know all the answers but that I have a plan, that I have done this before and that they can trust me.'

Although the surgeon does not know it, underpinning this explanation is probably the most important fact about being an effective communicator: it is not about the words that we use but the way that we deliver them. When asked what words she had actually used, the surgeon could not remember, but what she could describe were the emotions and values she wanted to convey: openness, honesty, trust, and competence. As will be discussed in Chapter 4, in a crisis situation, such as this one, our emotions take control, our brain senses a threat, which causes a flight (I just want this to be over), fight (I am not going to let anything bad happen to my son), or freeze (I can't cope with this right now) reaction. Jack's parents are scared and worried about their son. They are aware that whatever the surgeon has to say, it will not be good news. Their brain perceives the inevitability of bad news as a threat – their son's life could be at risk. So, before they can hear what is being said to them, they need to feel comforted and calmed, to feel that they are in the competent hands of someone they can trust to make the right decision for their son. Effective communication is never more important than in a crisis situation, when we feel as though we are drowning in an ocean of uncertainty and fear. At these times, a sense of emotional safety must be created (Van der Kolk, 2015). This happens not as the result of the words used but as a result of the way in which the words are delivered. What we respond to is the emotional message, 'You are safe with me', allowing the stress hormone cortisol to drain away from our body so that our brain allows us to relax.

'As surgeons, we are sometimes right and sometimes wrong', says Jack's surgeon, 'but we are never indecisive'.

This message of calm certainty can prevent difficult conversations from escalating into crisis situations. As professionals in education, health, or social care, we experience challenging conversations (although hopefully not about testicular torsions) on a daily basis. Effective communication is the key to developing a sense of emotional safety, to reducing the fight, flight, freeze response. And it is only when we are feeling emotionally safe that we can attend to what is being said.

Too much jargon – The Babel Fish Test

In his fictional work, *The Hitchhiker's Guide to the Galaxy* (2007), Douglas Adams explains that in order for hitchhikers travelling the galaxy to understand everything they hear, they should always have a babel fish in their ear:

> The Babel Fish is small yellow leech-like and probably the oddest thing in the universe…, and simultaneously translates from one spoken language to another. When inserted into the ear, its nutrition processes convert sound waves into brain waves, neatly crossing the language divide between any species you should happen to meet.

As professionals with years of experience, it is easy to forget that in difficult conversations the people we are talking with do not automatically understand the 'professional-speak' that we use and they do not have a babel fish in their ear to help them understand. We become so used to using acronyms and jargon – specialised vocabulary linked to a job or profession (Gallo, 2016) – that we no longer notice when we include it. If you are a parent who has been asked to come and talk to a class teacher, a carer who has been asked to come to hear the outcome of an appeal from a social worker, or a family member waiting to hear bad news from a doctor or nurse, you are already feeling anxious. While jargon is useful as a shortcut for intra-professional meetings – doctors and nurses, teachers and teaching assistants, social workers and support workers – it can act as a barrier to effective communication when talking to those outside the profession (Gallo, 2016). The surgeon in our case study understands this: it's 'about using language that everyone can understand rather than medical jargon'. If communication is to be effective, it must be accessible to all. In our book *True Partnerships in SEND* (2023), a colleague and I conducted interviews with parents of children with special educational needs and disabilities (SEND) to try to work out how partnerships working with professionals could be improved. Time and again parents talked about the barriers created by poor communication, as one of the fathers explained:

'I think that's one of the difficult elements of this … not understanding what is going on … you would get these explanations but you still wouldn't understand what they meant or you would get… some kind of medical terminology… Whereas, with Charlie we could just say, "Charlie I don't understand what you are talking about, can you just explain it in a more comprehensible way?" And

he would … he had the ability to communicate in a way that we understood. … That ability to communicate … is really fundamental and I think a lot of health-care professionals … were very poor at it. As parents you choose the people that you trust and often you trust them because you understand what they are communicating' (Extract from Interview, with permission, Green & Edwards, 2023).

When we talk about effective communication, we often talk about clarity – clarity of purpose, clarity of message – but clarity should begin with something more fundamental than this; it should begin with checking that we are speaking the same language, that everyone involved in the conversation can understand each other without needing a Babel Fish.

Activity: The Babel Fish Test

- Write down ten acronyms, abbreviations, or words specific to your profession and try to think of a way of explaining them to someone you have never met.
- When preparing for a difficult conversation, write down any jargon you think might be used beforehand and practise explaining it in no more than six words.

I believe everything your face is saying

Communication is about transmitting messages (Graber, 2003). How we transmit those messages depends on many things: on how we are feeling, on how others are feeling, on our body language, on our tone of voice, on our understanding of the situation, on the power dynamic, on how well we understand ourselves and others, on our relationship with the people we are talking to. What is surprising is that very little of our effectiveness as verbal communicators depends on the words we use. In his book *Silent Messages* (1972), Mehrabian explains that only 7% of how we understand what we hear depends on the words used, while 38% depends on the tone of voice and 55% depends on the facial expression of the person communicating with us. This is important for an effective communicator to know, especially when it comes to difficult conversations. How often do we spend hours formulating and re-formulating the exact words to use when we want to end a relationship, confront a colleague, talk to a parent? It turns out that we are focusing on the wrong thing.

When we are preparing for a difficult conversation, it is not the words we should be thinking about but what our face is saying, or what our tone of voice is implying. Mehrabian's research also showed that when the words and facial expression do not match, it is the facial expression that we will respond to rather than the words or tone of voice. So, if someone is saying, 'I *loved* your book on difficult conversations', but their facial expression shows that they disliked every word, then we will believe that they hated our book, however positive their words. The same is true of tone of voice when we are on the phone: we might not be able to see the expression on the face of the person we are talking to, but we will hear when the tone of voice does not match the words being used, and it is what is being implied by the tone that we will take away from the conversation. What people really think about this book is not important (or at least only to us), but believing that your son is in the hands of a capable, caring, and trustworthy surgeon could be life-changing.

Activity

- To help you think about facial expressions, try looking in the mirror and saying something enthusiastic when looking angry, something sad while looking happy, and something cross while looking sad.
- It's hard but it helps you to think about the message that your expressions are giving while you are talking.

Less is always more: The six-word rule

Six-word stories:

> Born a twin. Graduated only child.
> For sale: Baby's shoes, never worn.
> Torched the haystack. Found the needle.

> (www.6wordstories.net)

In just six words a whole story can be created. The meaning is clear; no further explanation is needed. This is how all effective communication should be shaped. Effective communication, whether verbal or in other forms, is about relaying information to get a point across. If either party does not understand the information conveyed, then the communication is not effective (Ratna, 2019).

In his book *Thinking, Fast and Slow* (2012) Nobel Prize winner Daniel Kahneman talks about the importance of avoiding cognitive strain, of reducing mental effort, for our audience.

'If you care about being thought credible and intelligent', he tells us, 'Do not use complex language where simpler language will do' (Kahneman, 2012: 110). If we must work hard to understand what someone is saying, we are going to stop listening while our brain tries to process what has just been said. Communication needs to have a clear purpose that can be expressed with as few words as possible. We already know that the words themselves have little to do with how we understand what is being said, so use as few as possible and make every word count. The indomitable Bernadine Healy, the first woman to become Head of the National Institutes of Health (NIH) in the USA in 1991, is said to have had a sign on her desk with the words STRONG VERBS, SHORT SENTENCES written on it in large letters. As head of the Red Cross in the USA, she was constantly frustrated by the barriers that were put up when she was trying to introduce change. The final sentence of one of her most famous quotations below could almost be a six-word story:

'It irritates me to be told how things have always been done. *I defy the tyranny of precedent.*'

Anyone who has had to battle inflexible, outdated systems in their organisation immediately knows what she means. Healy realised what most of us had yet to learn, that communication is powerful when it is concise and focuses on one issue at a time (Patterson et al., 2002). Never has this been more true than today; in this age of 24-hour information overload, when we are relentlessly bombarded by emails, phone messages, and social media updates, how do we choose what to read or listen to? We have all looked at a long WhatsApp message, groaned and scrolled up, or seen how thick a book is and put it back on the shelf, or received a wordy email which we add to our 'read later' and soon move to our 'never read' list. If we want people to listen or read what we are saying, we need to keep it short.

Activity

If you are preparing for a difficult conversation, try to summarise the aim of the conversation in six words.

Case study: A race to the finish

Anna is a primary school teacher who has been praised for the way in which she manages behaviour in her classroom. A recent Ofsted report has highlighted behaviour management as an area that needs improvement in the school. School governors are worried about the increase in challenging behaviours and have asked the headteacher to create a more robust behaviour policy as part of the school's improvement plan. She has asked Anna to make a ten-minute presentation to the governors to demonstrate effective practice. Anna knows the headteacher is depending on her to convince governors that the school can change and improve. Anna has spent hours in the evenings preparing clear slides and planning what she will say. She has practised at home in front of the mirror. As she stands up to deliver her presentation, Anna is nervous. She can feel her heart beating fast and her hands shaking. When she has finished speaking, she looks around the room. The governors are looking confused. She looks at her watch and realises that she has just delivered her ten-minute presentation in five minutes.

What happened?

We have all been in situations like Anna's where the pressure is on, when others depend on our words and our emotions run high. When this happens and adrenaline is coursing through our bodies, we either freeze and can think of nothing to say or, without knowing it, we talk as fast as possible. Anna is an experienced speaker; she stands in front of her class every day and explains complicated ideas. She knows how important it is to speak clearly, to slow down and ensure that her students understand what she is saying, but this is a different situation, a different audience with different expectations. When our job involves communication, it is easy to fall into the trap of believing that we can communicate effectively whatever the situation, that our communication skills are infinitely transferable. Speaking fast reflects excitement and passion, while speaking at a slower pace denotes importance, the belief that what we are saying really matters. We know that only 7% of what we say depends on the words we use, and we know that 37% of how we are understood depends on our tone of voice. If we are speaking very fast, our tone of voice is lost in an avalanche of words and we do not have time to assess how these words are being received (Moss, 2017). The school governors probably heard the passion in Anna's voice and would not have doubted her commitment, but they would not have been able to follow what she was saying because she was moving through the subject too fast. If the people listening to you are not experts in the field, they need time to process and understand what is being said. Talking at a slower pace allows for this.

Of course, there are times when speaking too slowly can detract from what we are trying to say, when the message gets lost in the gap between the words, where waiting for the next word becomes effortful, where the audience loses interest and begins to daydream about what to have for dinner or what they think will happen in the next episode of their favourite soap opera. Reflecting Kahneman's (2012) belief that fast intuitive thinking leads to creativity and spontaneity, Harkness (2020) believes that speaking fast evokes a sense of 'fun, optimism and agreeableness'. John F. Kennedy, President of the United States between 1961 and 1963, was famous for his fast speaking. In a normal conversation, we usually speak at between 120 and 130 words per minute. At his fastest, JFK was speaking at 362 words per minute. He was young and vibrant and new. That's what his ability to talk quickly implied. But in his inaugural speech, when he needed every word to count, when it was imperative that his message was clear and understood, when every sentence mattered, when he needed to be perceived as a confident, knowledgeable, and trustworthy world leader, he slowed right down to 96.5 words per minute. A study by Cascio Rizzo and Berger (2023) of 200 customer service phone calls found that customer satisfaction increased when the customer service reps slowed down their rate of articulation. Customers perceived the listeners to be more thoughtful and considered in their responses and, crucially, found them to be more empathetic. The importance of empathy will be discussed in the next chapter; it plays an important role in difficult conversations, engendering trust. In a difficult conversation, responding in a slow, considered manner makes those you have been listening to believe that their voice has been heard and that their views matter.

Communication is about having a conversation with your audience – whether you are standing in front of a crowd or the governors at a school or a video camera where you have no idea who will be watching. The best communicators bring their audience with them. As listeners we need to process the facial expression and tone of voice as well as the words we are listening to. This takes time and it demands cognitive effort (Kahneman, 2012) – if we talk too fast, our brains do not have time to process all the different parts of the information being transferred and will revert to interpreting the facial expressions and tone of voice, rather than hearing the content. Have you ever heard someone speak and realised afterwards that all you could remember was how you thought they were feeling – nervous or excited or angry – without remembering anything that they had said? This is often because the delivery was too fast.

In his TED Talk in Verona in 2016, Simon Lancaster talked about the effectiveness of rhyme when making a speech or a presentation. Rhyme makes things easier to remember and supports processing fluency (Lancaster, 2016). Perhaps a rhyme can also help us to remember to slow down when we speak:

'It should be all about the pace, not the look on your face.'

Activity

- Record yourself talking for one minute on your smartphone. Listen back and count the number of words you have said. (Even better is to use a tool that can convert your recording into written text.)
- Try to cut it right down to no more than 120 words per minute.

Case study: Know your audience

A lecturer has arranged a catch-up tutorial for two Muslim students who have missed a lecture on resilience due to celebrating Eid. It has been agreed that the lecturer will go through the lecture material with them to ensure that the students do not fall behind. The lecture explores academic understanding of resilience, making links to the evolutionary development of the brain. The students listen attentively but do not engage in discussion of the topic when given the opportunity to do so. When the lecture is finished, they thank the lecturer.

'Did you find it interesting?' she asks.

For a moment the students are silent, then one of them says, 'It was interesting, but you know that in our faith we do not believe that the brain developed this way. We believe that humans are unique and created by Allah.'

'We could have discussed that', says the lecturer. 'Why did you not bring it up when I asked if there was anything you would like to discuss?'

'Because in our country it is disrespectful to disagree with the teacher', explains the student.

Questions from this scenario

- How should the lecturer respond?
- What could the lecturer have done to better prepare?
- What could the lecturer have done to try and engage the students in conversation?

Communication is not 'one size fits all' (Ramsey, 2005: 172); everyone we meet and talk to has their own story, their own values, their own voice. This is very clear in the scenario above, where lecturers and students hold fundamentally different views. But this does not have to mean that our communication is faulty; it simply means that it is important to know who our audience is, what their experience is, and what is important to them. Knowledge is power and being interested in and finding out more about our audience creates trust and understanding. Communication is at its most effective when the people we are talking to believe that they matter to us, that they are significant (Flett, 2018). Parents of children with SEND trust professionals who understand that while for them a difficult conversation may be one of many from a heavy caseload, for the mother or father or carer standing in front of them, it is personal (Green & Edwards, 2023). Oprah Winfrey recognises this in her autobiography, *What I Know for Sure* (1988) when she talks about our human need to be heard and to believe that we are important.

When running a 'Let's Chat' group at a children's centre, we once made the mistake of talking to some Chinese parents about the benefits of vegetarianism. They had not been in the UK for long and looked astonished. 'If you have money, why do you not eat meat?' they asked. In China, meat is a luxury. Whatever our personal views on vegetarianism, this was not a good topic to choose as a focus for the conversation. In both this example and the scenario above, the professionals involved would have benefited from greater cultural awareness and a discussion with the participants. We should have done our homework. In hospitals older people often become upset when they are referred to by their first name, rather than as Mrs or Mr Brown. In difficult conversations the small things matter. Communication is not just about expressing ourselves; it is about understanding those who we want to understand us.

Activity

When you are preparing for a difficult conversation, write down three things you know about the person/people you will be talking to.

Communicating effectively by email and text

Whilst this chapter has focused mostly on verbal communication, we cannot ignore the fact that much of the way we communicate is through our phones, on social media, and by email. We have explored the idea that only 7% of the way that we understand verbal communication is linked to the words that are used; that we depend on facial expression and tone of voice to provide the context and build our understanding (Moss, 2017). In written communication, all of these extra cues are missing. It has never been easier to misunderstand the intent behind a message, and it happens all the time. As effective written communicators we need to try and compensate for the parts of our communication that will be missing.

'Are you free tomorrow morning?' could be interpreted in many ways. 'Do you have time for a coffee and a catch up?' 'Are you available for an important meeting?' 'It is time for a difficult conversation.'

As the sender of the message, make sure you give as much information as possible:

'Are you free tomorrow morning? I really want to tell you about my holiday.'

'Are you free tomorrow morning? If you are, I will book a room so that we can meet with the new team leader.'

'Are you free tomorrow? There is something important we need to discuss.'

In this work-heavy, time-poor world, texts, messages, and emails are often written while we are on our way to somewhere else. They are seen as a quick, efficient way to communicate – but it is important to ensure that quickness and efficiency are not synonymous with lacking in information and clarity. As the recipient it is often a good idea to ask for clarification: 'I am free. What did you have in mind?' or 'I am free but I'm not sure what you are thinking. Could you tell me?'

21

And if you want to try *to* help... there is always an emoji, the universal, cross-cultural, facial expression (Coyle & Carmichael, 2019).

Conclusion

Being an effective communicator is not just about speaking clearly. It involves many expressive and receptive skills, including self-awareness, emotional intelligence, and as much knowledge as possible about the audience. We must be aware of our body language, our facial expressions, and our intonation; we must be able to speak slowly enough for people to process what we are saying, but quickly enough to keep them interested and engaged. We must be able to read the their body language, expressions, and intonation and to adapt the way we communicate in response. We must sound confident but caring, speak with clarity and certainty, communicate because we want people to understand – not because we want to be heard. Communicating effectively can be complicated but is a crucial element of any difficult conversation.

Key takeaways

- Communicating is more about facial expression and tone of voice than about the words we use
- Always be clear, succinct, and jargon-free
- Be constantly aware of how quickly or slowly you are speaking
- Know your audience
- Show the person/people you are talking to that they matter to you

References

Adams, D. (2007). *The hitchhiker's guide to the galaxy.* London: Random House.

Cascio Rizzo, G.L., & Berger, J.A. (2023). The power of speaking slower. Available at SSRN.

Coyle, M.A. & Carmichael, C.L. (2019). Perceived responsiveness in text messaging: The role of emoji use. *Computers in Human Behavior, 99,* 181–189.

Flett, G. (2018). *The psychology of mattering: Understanding the human need to be significant.* London: Academic Press.

Gallo, K. (2016). Understanding professional jargons. *Educational Psychology, 52*(10), 157–163.

Garrod, S., & Pickering, M.J. (2004). Why is conversation so easy? *Trends in Cognitive Sciences, 8*(1), 8–11.

Green, H., & Edwards, B. (2023). *True partnerships in SEND: Working together to give children, families and professionals a voice.* London: Routledge.

Hall J.A., & Morella, A. (2020). Connecting everyday talk and time alone to global well-being. *Human Communication Research, 46*, 594–619.

Harkness, T. (2020). *10 rules for talking: An expert's guide to mastering difficult conversations.* London: Kings Road Publishing.

Herrando, C., & Constantinides, E. (2021). Emotional contagion: A brief overview and future directions. *Frontiers in Psychology, 12*, 712606.

Kahneman, D. (2012). *Thinking, fast and slow.* London: Penguin.

Lancaster, S. (2016). TEDx Verona. https://www.youtube.com/watch?v=bGBamf WasNQ.

Lindon, J. (2016). *Understanding child development: 0–8 years.* London: Hodder.

Mehrabian, A. (1972). *Silent messages: Implicit communication of emotions and attitudes.* Belmont, CA: Wadsworth Publishers.

Morelli, S.A., Rameson, L.T., & Lieberman, M.D. (2014). The neural components of empathy: Predicting daily prosocial behavior. *Social Cognitive and Affective Neuroscience, 9*, 39–47.

Moss, B. (2017). *Communication skills in health and social care.* London: Sage.

Mukherji, P., & Dryden, L. (2014). *Foundations of early childhood. principles and practice.* London: Sage.

Patterson, K. Grenny, R., McMillan, & Switzler, A. (2002). *Crucial conversations: Tools for talking when stakes are high.* New York: McGraw-Hill.

Piferi R.L., & Lawler K.A. (2006). Social support and ambulatory blood pressure: An examination of both receiving and giving. *International Journal of Psychophysiology, 62*, 328–335.

Ramsey, R.D. (Ed.) (2005). *Lead, follow, or get out of the way: How to be a more effective leader in today's schools.* Thousand Oaks, CA: Corwin Press.

Ratna, H. (2019). The importance of effective communication in healthcare practice. *Harvard Public Health Review, 23*, 1–6.

Rogers, C. (1951). *Client-centered therapy.* Cambridge, MA: The Riverside Press.

Rosengren, K. (2006). *Communication and Introduction.* London: Sage.

Stone, D., Patton, B., & Heen, S. (2021). *Difficult conversations. How to discuss what matters most.* London: Penguin.

Van der Kolk, B. (2015). *The body keeps the score. Mind brain and body in the transformation of trauma.* London: Penguin Books.

Winfrey, O. (1988). *What I know for sure.* London: Macmillan.

3
Are you really listening?

Introduction

Listening so that someone feels heard is probably one of the hardest things we ever have to do. In the previous chapter we explored the idea that only 7% (Moss, 2017) of how we understand what is said to us depends on the words used. The rest depends on facial expression, tone of voice, and body language. A good listener attends not only to what is being said but also to what is *not* being said, and must understand the importance of silence, of the pauses between words. In difficult conversations where risks are high and emotions are raw, it is easy to interpret what we see and hear through the lens of our unconscious bias (Gladwell, 2013), making the dialogue fit with what we want to believe, not with what is actually being said. If we do not listen properly, we will only be having half a conversation. But conversations are complicated and multifaceted (Weizsäcker, 2023), and listening is a complicated and multifaceted process. This chapter explores the skills, qualities, and ideas that can help us all to become better listeners.

Case study: Perception – The voice from the back of the car

It was a hot sunny day, and I (Becky) was driving our 5-year-old daughter and 4-year-old son to the beach. It was a short journey, but it was a hot day and the going was slow – everyone was heading to the beach. In the front of the car I was chatting to my friend who had joined us for the day, and in the back of the car the children were chatting, sometimes to each other, sometimes to themselves. Suddenly my son leant forward and, raising his voice above the chat and the noise of the car, enunciating his words very slowly, he said: 'Mum... will … you... just... for... one... moment... in... your... life... listen... to... ME'.

DOI: 10.4324/9781003433248-4

The force of his words took me by surprise, mostly because it felt to me as though I spent all my days doing nothing *but* listening to him and his sister. Getting them ready for school, playing with them, reading to them, laughing with them, drying their tears, easing their fears... to me there seemed to be no part of any day when I did not think about and listen to my children. And yet here was my 4-year-old son telling me that, despite all this, he felt neither heard nor listened to.

Before we start to listen, we need to understand that our perceptions are personal and individual; that how one person interprets words or actions is never the same as how another person interprets them. When we listen, it is important to remember that the person we are listening to probably understands the world very differently from us. Listening is about understanding that we all have and believe our own version of what happens, and it is therefore possible for two completely opposing views to be true at the same time (Stone, 2011). For example:

My son believes that I never listen to him, and I believe that I never stop listening to him.

There is no point in trying to prove who is wrong and who is right in this situation, or in any situation; the truth is that we are both right. But instead of trying to prove this, what is important is to try and understand each other's stories (Stone, 2011; Patterson et al., 2012). Why did my son believe I didn't listen to him? What made him feel as though he had no voice? In a difficult conversation listening is the key to unravelling absolute and often opposing certainties (Patterson et al., 2012) and to changing perceptions from individual to shared.

What I did begin to realise from my son, sitting in the back of the car, is the difference between being 'in the same space' and being 'present' (I was in the car but not attending to what he was saying), between authenticity and superficiality. (I responded as though I was listening, but my mind was somewhere else.) What I was beginning to understand was the difference between hearing and really listening.

Activity

At the end of the day (perhaps before you go to sleep) think back on one conversation you had. Choose three adjectives to sum up how the other person was feeling, three words to sum up what they were hoping to get out of the conversation, and three words to sum up what you were hoping to get out of the conversation. Finally, sum up in six words what the outcome of the situation was. Consider whether the outcome was useful to everyone? If it was, congratulations, you have had a successful conversation. If it wasn't, what went wrong?

Hearing vs listening

Lundsteen (1979) describes hearing as a physical act and listening as a mental one. While hearing is about receiving and processing sounds, listening is about making sense of and assigning meaning to what we hear. While hearing is automatic (without noticing that we are doing it, we hear birds singing, cars driving past), listening demands cognitive effort. To listen we must be able to attend to and focus on what is being said (In the car that day, I needed to stop chatting with my friend and switch my attention to my son). Listening involves conscious decisions and choices. It gives clear messages (I am choosing to concentrate on what you are telling me rather than texting my friend) and can be the difference between feeling validated and valued or feeling powerless and voiceless.

In difficult conversations, nothing is more important than our capacity to listen.

Activity

As you are getting out of your car or walking to work, listen to what is happening around you and try to identify three sounds that you wouldn't usually be aware of.

Listening superheroes

It is hard to imagine that something as theoretically passive as listening could be called 'active'. But the skills involved in listening can be as demanding emotionally as a marathon is physically. Listening is active because to do it properly, we must become actively involved in the process: being present, concentrating, responding. If a difficult conversation is to be successful, then all those involved must be on a listening journey towards a shared story where differences can be resolved and compromises reached (Patterson et al., 2012). And like every journey, there are hazards, pitfalls, and detours along the way.

The list of skills involved with being an effective listener can feel endless. We must be able to listen with: patience, openness, and a desire to understand (Covey, 2020); we must be interested, non-judgemental, and have the ability to be comfortable with silence (Ramsey, 2005); we must constantly check how others are feeling, be able to create a sense of emotional safety and build trusting relationships (Patterson et al., 2012); we must be able to pay attention, have emotional intelligence, and possess the ability to reflect back and summarise what we have heard (Fisher & Ury, 1991). Anyone who can do this all the time with everyone they meet is probably a fictional character. But many of the skills listed above are contained in the work of American psychologist Carl Rogers, who introduced the idea of person-centred listening in 1958.

Person-centred listening: Congruence, empathy, and unconditional positive regard

Rogers believed that the most important thing to do when we listen is to build a trusting relationship by listening with congruence, empathy, and unconditional positive regard.

Congruence – listening with genuineness and authenticity.

'Listening is only powerful and effective if it is authentic. Authenticity means that you are listening because you are curious and because you care' (Stone, 2011: 90).

If we remove the masks we often wear as professionals, if we are willing to acknowledge and show our emotions to others, we become a person rather than a professional (Cooper et al., 2013) and are more likely to be perceived as someone who can be trusted.

Empathy – understanding things from the other person's point of view, entering into their private perceptual world, sensing their feelings, and being aware of the meaning that is real to them in the moment (Cooper et al., 2013). Baron-Cohen (2011) describes two types of empathy: cognitive – our ability to understand another's thoughts and feelings; and affective – our ability to respond to another person's mental state with appropriate emotion.

Unconditional positive regard – caring about someone with no conditions attached (Cooper et al., 2013), accepting them non-judgementally for who they are, with no pre-conceived ideas about who they should be.

Many families and children we work with in education, health, and social care are struggling in different ways, and often they have never felt listened to, never felt that they have a voice in the decisions made about them. By accepting them for who they are, not who we think they should be, by listening to their stories and celebrating every success, however small, we are able to help them start believing in themselves. Listening with congruence means that they begin to trust us, listening with empathy means that they feel understood, and listening with unconditional positive regard means that they feel empowered.

Case study: Tina and Soria

Tina is 17 and has a 2-year-old daughter, Soria. Tina is a lone parent and does not have contact with Soria's dad, Tom, who is expecting a baby with his new girlfriend. A caseworker from her local children's centre has been working with Tina, trying to get her to spend more time interacting and playing with Soria. Whatever time of day the caseworker goes round to the house, morning or afternoon, Soria is always in a wet nappy and a T-shirt, sitting in front of the TV surrounded by toys, whilst Tina is sitting on the sofa texting. They never seem to leave the house except to go shopping when Soria will be in the buggy with an iPad so that she can watch cartoons. The caseworker has tried to suggest taking Soria to the park, but Tina says she does not feel safe there because Tom's friends often hang out there, smoking and drinking. The caseworker has also suggested that she join a parent and toddler group in the church hall, but Tina says it is full of 'yummy mummies' who ignore her. One morning at 10.30am, Tina turns up in the children's centre. She is pushing Soria in the buggy. Soria is dressed and wearing a clean nappy (still holding the iPad). Tina is smiling and looks proud. She tells the caseworker proudly that she has 'been down the arcade' on the slot machines with Soria all morning and that they had breakfast together in the cafe.

How should the caseworker respond?

Obviously, an amusement arcade is not the best place for a 2-year-old to spend their morning. But using congruence, empathy, and unconditional positive regard to frame her response, the caseworker listened whilst Tina told her everything about their adventure. The caseworker praised Tina for getting Soria up and dressed, and for catching the bus. She said how good it was that they had eaten breakfast together (**unconditional positive regard**) and commented on how hard it must have been to remember to bring nappies and bottles of milk (**empathy**). She asked what they had eaten for breakfast and what Soria and Tina's favourite thing about the morning had been and said how important it was that they had been having fun together (**unconditional positive regard**). She also said how much it meant to her that Tina had come to tell her all about it, that it made her feel special (**congruence**). And then she added that while Tina was in the centre, perhaps they could grab a cup of tea and a sandwich in the cafe and then go to the messy play session that was running in the centre together and that now she knew the bus timetable, perhaps they could go to a park in town together next week and she would bring a picnic (**seizing the day**).

Why we listen

The key to listening effectively is to know why we are doing it. In life our actions are only impactful when we are clear about their purpose. This is also true of listening. We listen because we want to try and understand what someone else is thinking and feeling; we listen in order to understand, not to be understood (Covey, 2020). In this self-absorbed, self-promoting social media world, it is important to remember that listening is not 'all about me'; it is 'all about the other person'.

We all have those friends who appear to listen, when really all they want to do is talk about themselves.

You: It's been a hard week. My mum has been in hospital because she fell down the stairs and broke her arm.

Friend: Oh, I know. It was the same for me when my daughter fell over, and we had to take her to hospital. We had to wait hours in A&E.

You: Our son has decided to go and study in Canada. I'm excited for him, but it is so far away. I will miss him.

Friend: Canada's great. We travelled around Canada there in a campervan a few years ago. It was one of our favourite holidays.

You: My father-in-law has just been diagnosed with Parkinson's. It's going to be very hard for my mother-in-law to look after him. I'm not sure that he will be able to stay living at home.

Friend: Our daughter has just started working with people with Parkinson's. The manager is so impressed with how quickly she is learning everything. They've already said she should apply for the assistant manager's job when it comes up.

These conversations are hard because the listening is out of sync with the messaging. Both of us will walk away feeling frustrated and unheard – and will probably make a mental note to never meet each other for coffee when having a bad day, or maybe ever again! In difficult and important conversations, we look for understanding of the unspoken emotions behind our words: worry about my mum, sadness about my son, fear for the future for my parents-in-law. But my friend is concentrating on finding a platform for her own story. Normal conversational and listening cues: tone of voice, facial expression, body language, are not being responded to. My friend does not hear my need for emotional containment or comfort, and I do not give her space to talk about what is important to her. When messages and responses are misaligned like this, when we do not listen with the intent to understand but with the intent to reply or just to tell our own story, difficult conversations will fail (Covey, 2020). Listening should open a channel to help us construct meaning (Dubberly & Pangaro, 2009), to find the shared story (Patterson et al., 2012) that can move a conversation forward. If the way we listen is shaped by cross-purpose rather than clear purpose, it will never be effective.

Activity

Take time in a conversation. Before you reply to someone, check why it is you are about to say something. If it is simply because you want to tell your own story, *stop* and re-calibrate. Will telling your story move the conversation forward? If not, don't tell it. Instead, respond to the story of the person you are listening to.

If you trust me, I will trust you

Before people feel listened to, they must be able to trust the listener. This is what motivated Carl Rogers and was clear in the case study in the previous chapter where a surgeon must discuss a complicated and potentially life-changing operation with the parents of a young child. Through listening with congruence and empathy, the surgeon was able to create a trusting relationship and a sense of emotional safety in a very short space of time. In difficult conversations, those being listened to must believe that their feelings are securely held and contained by the listener (Van der Kolk, 2015). When this happens, a trusting relationship develops and a sense of emotional safety is created (Patterson et al., 2012). It is only when emotional safety has been established that we can begin to process information. In the case study above, when Tina came into the children's centre, she had to believe that her caseworker would listen to her and value what she had achieved. When we listen we must show that we have the other person's best interests in mind, that we respect their opinion and trust their motives (Patterson et al., 2012). If we do this, no one needs to feel attacked or humiliated, and there is no need to become defensive. If we create a state of trust, we open the door to meaningful communication (Gladwell, 2021) and difficult conversations become easier.

The listening superpower

As seen from the beginning of this chapter, the list of skills and qualities needed to be a good listener can seem endless, like something that only a superhero could possess. Truthfully, the ability to listen effectively, to create certainty where there is uncertainty, understanding where there is suspicion, clarity where there is confusion, is a sort of superpower. The good news is that with practice, it can become a superpower that we all possess. Below is a checklist of what we need to consider before, during, and after a difficult conversation to ensure that we are really listening and that others feel listened to.

Preparation

Timing

Consider when the conversation will happen. There are certain times of the day best avoided. Be aware that we are normally at our most alert mid-morning and at our least alert mid-afternoon (Walker, 2017) – but everyone has pinch points in their day, so try to find a mutually convenient time, not just the time that works best for you. This gives everyone some control and shows that you are all equal partners in the conversation.

Location

Where will the conversation take place? Try to find somewhere calm and quiet. This can be difficult in a busy classroom, hospital ward, or living room on a home visit, but is essential if everyone is to focus on the conversation and feel emotionally safe. If possible, offer a choice: 'Would you rather meet in my office or chat here?' This gives the message that you want everyone to feel comfortable.

Allocate enough time

Make sure that you block out enough time in your calendar to give your full attention to the conversation. Listening takes time; it is not something you can dip in and out of between meetings. For people to feel listened to, they need to believe that they matter to you (Schlossberg, 2008), that you are interested in and care about what they have to say. If you are constantly looking at the clock or distracted because you are thinking about your next meeting, the message you are giving is that the conversation is not important to you, that you are not interested in what they have to say. Lack of time is constantly highlighted as a reason why parents in schools and patients in hospitals don't feel listened to (Green & Edwards, 2023; Gladwell, 2005). Remember the surgeon? Despite the necessity for speed to ensure the operation could take place as quickly as possible, the surgeon made Jack's parents feel as though they had time to speak, and she had time to listen.

Where will you sit?

Think about power dynamics. Can you place chairs so that you can sit next to each other rather than opposite each other? In their book *Getting to YES* (1991), international negotiators Fisher and Ury explain that even in high-level negotiations, the act of getting representatives from opposing teams, organisations, or countries to sit side by side at a table, rather than sitting opposite each other, has an impact on reaching a solution. As simple as it sounds, it is also important to think about the chairs you will be sitting on. If possible, they should both/all be the same height. But if this is not possible, ensure that the person invited to participate in the conversation can sit on the higher chair. Positioning gives subliminal messages: we are equal partners in this conversation; your views are just as important as mine. When stakes are high, every message counts (Patterson et al., 2012).

Purpose of the conversation

Clarity is key

Take time to think about what it is you are hoping to get from the conversation (Patterson et al., 2012). Remember the six-word rule: if you can't summarise what you are trying to say in six words, you are not being clear enough.

What do you want to achieve; what do you not want to happen?

Think of the three things you really want to gain from the conversation and three things you really don't want to happen; if you think of these beforehand, you will notice if the conversation is moving away from its focus and, more importantly, you will be aware if things are going wrong and can prevent everything from spiralling out of control.
   I want to:

- Get the family to agree to Grandad going home from hospital with support
- Link them up with support services
- Agree a date for him to go home

   I don't want to:

- Show that I am frustrated with their desire to keep him in hospital
- Seem like I have all the power
- Force them to agree to something they do not want

During the conversation

Listen

Listen with the intent to understand, not to be understood (Covey, 2020).

Consider body language

Remember that words are only 7% of what we understand when we listen (Moss, 2017). Be aware of facial expressions, tone of voice (are you sounding angry, patronising, judgemental), and body language (lean forward into the conversation rather than sit back with your arms crossed). It is easy to slip back into body language that is closed and unwelcoming, so keep checking.

Check how everyone is feeling

A sense of emotional safety is essential if conversations are to be honest and a trusting relationship is to develop (Patterson et al., 2012). This is true for everyone, including yourself. Analyse your emotions before bringing them into the conversation (Stone, 2011). If you notice that you or others seem to be getting overwhelmed, pause and take a break. The best way to gauge is through listening with your eyes as well as your ears (Patterson et al., 2012). Listen for the emotions behind the words and the unspoken messages from gestures and body language.

Be comfortable with silence

This is perhaps the most difficult thing I have had to learn. It is often the time when we are silent in a conversation that communication is at its most powerful. I am a naturally chatty person (just ask my husband). I am someone who will try to fill every moment with words. My days are flooded with unnecessary sentences, but in difficult conversations silence is crucial for understanding (Stone, 2011). Just as the singer/songwriter Leonard Cohen describes the cracks in everything being how the light gets in, so in difficult conversations the silence is how understanding creeps in.

'Don't be afraid of silence' is the advice a friend who works in a hospice gave me when I was talking with him about difficult conversations.

'But how do you stop yourself from talking', I asked. 'Silence is so uncomfortable.'

'Practice', he says. 'If you practise enough, it stops feeling uncomfortable. But one of the things I do is begin an internal monologue with myself. In my head, I fill the silence with words – shut up, don't talk, silence is good.'

And I know now that he is right: silence is probably one of the most important parts of any conversation. It is processing time, time for everyone to gather their thoughts and to prepare for the next part of the discussion.

Reflect back, paraphrase, and summarise

Restate what you have heard (Patterson et al., 2012). This acknowledges and validates what has been said, shows the other person that you have been listening, and ensures that you have understood correctly. For example, 'So, what I'm hearing is …'. 'Can I just check that I have understood this right …?'

Build trust

Listen non-judgementally – this will happen if you listen with congruence, empathy, and unconditional positive regard (Rogers, 1958) (see previous section).

Make eye contact

Eye contact shows that you are listening and attending to what is being said. The people you are with may choose to look away, but make sure that when they look back, you are still looking at them, and hold their gaze. It shows that they are at the centre of the conversation and that what they say matters. It gives the message that you are listening and concentrating on what they are saying, and it helps you to remain 'present' in the conversation (Fisher & Ury, 1991).

Be clear

Avoid using long sentences. Make sure that every word counts and that there is no confusion in your message. Begin by setting out what everyone is hoping to achieve from the conversation. Remember that the point of a difficult conversation is not to be liked but to be clear and find solutions (Stone, 2011).

Summarise

Before the conversation ends, remember to summarise what has been discussed and decided. It is easy to forget to do this when emotions have been running high, but focusing on the facts – 'This is what we have discussed', 'This is what has been decided', 'Is there anything else you want to add?' – can de-escalate a potentially explosive situation.

Decide if you want someone else to be there with you

Would it help to have someone there to jump in if people become overwhelmed, to ensure that you have heard what is said correctly and to act as mediator if things become heated or polarised?

After the conversation

Difficult conversations do not end when we walk out of the room or away from the discussion. We carry on processing them internally, often for days: *Did I react correctly? Did I really listen? Have I understood what was said?* If you have regular supervision, you will have the chance to talk it all through, but there are other things that can help immediately afterwards.

Talk it through with a trusted colleague or friend

Before the conversation takes place, identify someone whose opinion you trust and who you feel comfortable with. Explain the situation to them and ask if you could go for a coffee afterwards. If it is agreed beforehand, it will not feel as though you are burdening them.

Write down the key points

It is always better for thoughts to be out rather than in. The process of writing is cathartic and can help to clarify what you heard and what you think about it.

Go for a walk

If a conversation has been hard, if we have felt threatened by what has been said or implied, our brain believes us to be under attack and reverts to the fight, flight, freeze response. To think clearly, we need to get rid of excess energy, and exercise is the best way to do this. We probably can't go for a run or play a game of football in the middle of the day, but we can take ten minutes to go for a walk, even if it is only round the block. This is processing time, time to reflect – a ten-minute walk can save hours of agonising.

Beware!

While you are trying to listen to and engage with the conversation, watch out for mental traps and detours. Difficult conversations can feel threatening, and our over-protective brain tries to get us out of threatening situations in whatever way it can, even if that is only inside our heads.

Signs of stress

Don't forget to check in with how you are feeling: Is your heart rate increasing? Are you finding it hard to concentrate? If you are, you are moving into flight, fight, freeze. Pause the conversation, take deep breaths, and stand up for a few minutes. It will give everyone time to recharge their batteries before launching back into the conversation.

Mind-wandering

Be aware that your mind might wander. Defined as unguided attention (Irving, 2016; Irving & Thompson, 2018), mind-wandering is something that we all experience: it is thought that our minds wander because we are under-stimulated by the subject at hand (Shepherd 2019). In difficult conversations this can be particularly dangerous. We may perceive the other person's story to be littered with seemingly long-winded and irrelevant details, but we need to stay focused. Sometimes it is in the unravelling of irrelevancies, in the weight of seemingly unimportant details, that we can work out the root cause of a problem. As soon as you realise that you have been lost in other thoughts, ask for the last few sentences to be repeated. For example: 'Sorry, could you just say that again? I want to check that I have understood.'

Emotion contagion

When we are talking and interacting with others, we often begin to mimic their actions, and at our most empathetic we feel what they are feeling. This is known as emotional contagion and occurs when we synchronise with the emotional state of the person we are interacting with (Herrando & Constantinides, 2021). In conversations, it is a subconscious reflex, showing that we understand what the other person is experiencing. Try to be aware of when this is happening. While it helps us to listen with empathy, it can also prevent us from remaining objective.

Bias

Bias is an integral part of who we are and how we perceive the world (Kahneman, 2011). Without knowing it we listen out for statements that confirm our story and what we believe to be true. So, check for bias in your understanding of what has been said and, if you feel that you have not listened objectively, try to go back to the topic before the conversation ends.

Conclusion

Listening is a skill. It takes concentration, energy, focus, and preparation. It demands us to be empathetic, caring, and self-aware. We must be consistently attentive and present in the moment while being aware of the subliminal messages we might be transmitting and are receiving. We must recognise the power of silence and hear what isn't said. We must pay attention to body language, gestures, facial expressions, and tone of voice in both ourselves and those we are listening to. And we must do all of this without letting our emotions take control. It is not easy, but if we do it well, if we learn the skills and develop strategies to become effective listeners, difficult conversations will become easier, and no one will need to be shouting out from the back of the car.

Key takeaways

- Don't be afraid of silence
- Listening is about understanding, not being understood
- Listen with empathy, congruence, and unconditional positive regard
- Recognise your biases
- Remember that it is possible for two seemingly opposing views to be true at the same time

References

Baron-Cohen, S. (2011). *Zero degrees of empathy: A new theory of human cruelty.* London: Penguin/Allen Lane.

Brown, B. (2013). *Daring greatly: How the courage to be vulnerable transforms the way we live, love, parent and lead.* London: Penguin.

Cooper, M., O'Hara, M., & Schmid, P. (2013). *The handbook of person-centred psychotherapy and counselling.* New York: Bloomsbury Academic.

Covey, S.R. (2020). *The 7 habits of highly effective people.* New York: Simon & Schuster.

Dubberly, H., & Pangaro, P. (2009). What is conversation? How can we design for effective conversation? *Interactions Magazine, 16*(4), 22–28.

Fisher, R., & Ury, W., with Patton, B. (Ed.) (1991). *Getting to YES. Negotiating agreement without giving in.* New York: Houghton Mifflin.

Gladwell, M. (2005). *Blink. The power of thinking without thinking.* London: Penguin.

Gladwell, M. (2021). *Talking to strangers.* London: Penguin.

Green, H., & Edwards, B. (2023). *True partnerships in SEND: Working together to give children, professionals and families a voice.* London: Routledge.

Held, M., Minculescu, A., Rieger, J.W., & Borst, J.P. (2024). Preventing mind-wandering during driving: Predictions on potential interventions using a cognitive model. *International Journal of Human-Computer Studies, 181*, 103164.

Herrando, C., & Constantinides, E. (2021). Emotional contagion: A brief overview and future directions. *Frontiers in Psychology, 12*, 712606.

Irving, Z.C. (2016). Mind-wandering is unguided attention: Accounting for the 'purposeful' wanderer. *Philosophical Studies, 173*, 547–571.

Irving, Z.C., & Thompson, E. (2018). The philosophy of mind-wandering. In *Oxford handbook of spontaneous thought.* Oxford University Press.

Kahneman, D. (2011). *Thinking, fast and slow.* New York: Allen Lane.

Levinson, W., Roter, D.L., Mullooly, J.P., Dull, V.T., & Frankel, R.M. (1997). Physician-patient communication: The relationship with malpractice claims among primary care physicians and surgeons. *Jama, 277*(7), 553–559.

Lundsteen, S. (1979). *Listening: Its impact on reading and the other language arts.* Urbana, IL: Clearing House on Language and Communication Skills.

Moss, B. (2017). *Communication skills in health and social care.* London: Sage.

Patterson, K., Grenny, J., McMillan, R., & Switzler, A. (2012). *Crucial conversations: Tools for talking when stakes are high.* New York: McGraw-Hill.

Ramsey, R.D. (Ed.) (2005). *Lead, follow, or get out of the way: How to be a more effective leader in today's schools.* Thousand Oaks, CA: Corwin Press.

Randall, J., Hanson, M., & Nassrelgrgawi, A. (2022). Staying focused when nobody is watching: Self-regulatory strategies to reduce mind wandering during self-directed learning. *Applied Psychology, 71*(4), 1428–1464.

Rogers, C. (1958). The characteristics of a helping relationship. *Personnel and Guidance Journal, 37*(1), 6–16.

Shepherd, J. (2019). Why does the mind wander? *Neuroscience of Consciousness, 2019*(1), p.niz014.

Schlossberg, N. (2008). *Overwhelmed: Coping with life's ups and downs* (2nd ed.). Lanham, MD: Evans.

Stone, D. (2011). *Difficult Conversations: How to discuss what matters most.* London: Penguin.

Van der Kolk, B. (2015). *The body keeps the score: Brain, mind, and body in the transformation of trauma.* London: Penguin.

Walker, M. (2017). *Why we sleep: Unlocking the power of sleep and dreams.* London: Simon & Schuster.

Weizsäcker, G. (2023). *Misunderstandings: False beliefs in communication.* Open Book Publishers. DOI: 10.11647/OBP.0367.

4

How to take the 'difficult' out of difficult conversations

Introduction

Conversations that involve messages that no one wants to give or receive are intrinsically difficult. No one wants to be the person who delivers bad news: a special educational needs co-ordinator having to tell a family that their child might have a disability, a nurse or doctor having to tell a patient that they have a terminal illness, a social worker having to persuade a victim of domestic abuse to move to a refuge far from friends and family. At some point in our professional and private lives we will have to have a difficult conversation. Using the communication and listening skills discussed in the previous chapters, this chapter explores why some conversations can seem so difficult and what we can do to reset and reshape expectations and outcomes, so that difficult conversations become useful and effective discussions.

Why do we have conversations?

It is suggested that we began to use verbal conversation as a means to communicate when we began to use our hands for skills such as making flints and building fires (Dunbar, 1996). Before this we had used touch and physical interactions to communicate: stroking and delousing each other like chimpanzees do today. Whilst stroking and delousing provide concrete signs of affection, interpreting gestures, expressions, and words is much harder and can more easily lead to misunderstandings, but there are some benefits. The more abstract nature of conversation enables us to maintain many more social relationships than was the case when we depended on touch (the average person is able to maintain 150 social relationships; (Dunbar, 1996)), and to enjoy hours of chat, gossip, and laughter. But conversations are also strewn with difficulties; they can be fragmentary or lacking in context, are

DOI: 10.4324/9781003433248-5

often unpredictable and demand that we multi-task, planning how to respond whilst we are still listening to what is being said. We must work out when is socially appropriate to speak (usually we begin to speak 0.5 seconds before the other person has finished) and who to address if there is more than one person (Pickering & Garrod, 2004). It is not surprising that even before they become difficult, conversations can be emotionally exhausting.

What makes conversations difficult?

Often what makes conversation seem difficult has more to do with us than with anyone else. We worry about how we might be perceived, whether we can be assertive enough, what the implications will be for us if the conversation goes wrong (Stone et al., 2023). Worrying about these things means that we might miss crucial parts of the conversation or concentrate on the wrong thing, focusing on small details rather than on the bigger picture.

But we are only one part of any conversation; we must also be aware of the impact of what we say on others. Emotions can build up throughout a conversation intrinsically – internal responses to what is being discussed – and extrinsically – mirroring the emotions of the others in the conversation (Barsade et al., 2018). This results in a cumulative build-up of emotions that can make having a difficult conversation feel like walking through a minefield. We never know if something we do or say might trigger an emotional explosion. And what happens then?

How to deal with an emotional explosion

Often the subjects we are discussing will feel threatening or uncomfortable for the other people involved. This leads to hostility, anger, frustration, and defensiveness (Fisher & Ury, 2011). If there is nowhere else for these emotions to go, there is a good chance that they will all land on you. It is important to prepare yourself for this, think about how you will respond, and what you will do if someone gets angry. International negotiators Roger Fisher and William Ury advise allowing people to let off steam. They believe that giving them the opportunity to vent, airing grievances, enables them to release negative emotions, allowing psychological release. Prepare yourself to listen to the explosion calmly, without judgement or interruption, until everything is out in the open. Once the outburst is over, your role is to recognise and acknowledge what has happened:

'It is obvious that you feel very strongly about this and that it matters to you. Let's see if we can find a way to stop you feeling so worried. Shall we start with …?'

Once the emotions are out of the way, the focus of the conversation can be returned to its original focus. The best way to remain calm is to keep reminding yourself that they are angry about what has happened and how it has made them feel; they are not angry at you.

There have been many colleagues who did not agree with my (Becky's) leadership or management style, who felt aggrieved at something I had unknowingly said or done. Time has taught me to tackle this head on, to put on my emotional armour and to sit down with them and listen to their side of the story. I let them tell me everything they perceive as problematic, selfish, or hurtful in what I have done. I try to listen without defending myself until they have finished. I thank them for having the courage to tell me all these things and ask if we can go through them together and work out what went wrong. By breaking down each accusation into its constituent parts, I show them that I have listened to what they have said. It is important to accept that their perception is different from mine, that their story is as true to them as mine is to me. We each have our own version of what happened – they know things about the situation that I don't know, and I know things that they don't know (Stone et al, 2023). Acknowledging that things could have been done differently is not an admission of guilt but an acceptance that most problems have more than one solution. Anger and resentment are usually caused by misunderstandings and misinterpretations, by lack of clarity of intentions. A conversation can be a way of exploring what went wrong and where the misunderstanding began. We cannot step out of who we are nor undo what has been done, but we can learn to understand each other better. It is important not to try to get the other person to like you; the conversation is not about how others perceive us (Stone et al., 2023). Once the emotions and grievances have been aired, we can then focus on facts and rebuilding a broken relationship, professionally if not personally.

'Freed from the burden of unexpressed emotions, people will become more likely to focus on the problem' (Fisher & Ury, 2011: 74).

This is true in every scenario.

Making difficult conversations less difficult

⚲ Case study: Ashly

Ashly is in Year 10 and is completing 10 GCSEs, including combined science. Until this year Ashly has been a confident and popular student who does well academically. This year her personal tutor has noticed Ashly becoming withdrawn. She often looks tired, with dark rings under her eyes, and during breaks she will sit by herself reading. She tells her tutor that she is feeling anxious and sometimes finds it hard to get out of bed in the morning. She would like to give up her combined science GCSE, but she knows that her parents will not let her because they want her to study medicine at university. Ashly has unwillingly agreed to a meeting with her tutor and her parents at the end of a school day to discuss this further. The tutor has booked a room off the main hall where the noise of children leaving to go home can be clearly heard.

The conversation between the family and the tutor

Tutor:	Thank you for coming to this meeting. I am Emily Greenrow, Ashly's tutor.
Dad:	Thank you for arranging the meeting Miss Greenrow; it has been hard to take the time off work in the afternoon, but our daughter's education must come first.
Tutor:	Great. I just wanted to discuss a few concerns we have about Ashly.
Dad:	We have no concerns about Ashly. She helps at home and she works hard.
Tutor:	Yes, Ashly is a very able student but this year she seems to be finding it more difficult.
Dad:	Of course it is more difficult. GCSEs are not easy. But we are sure she will get good grades. Just like her brother.
Tutor:	The problem is that Ashly is feeling overwhelmed by the work. Is there anything you would like to say Ashly?

(Ashly looks at the floor and says nothing.)

Mum (sounding tearful):   It has been hard for Ashly these last few months. My mother has had a hip replacement operation. She is staying with us until she is better. We had to give her Ashly's room, so Ashly is sleeping on a mattress in her brother's room. He is often up late playing on his PlayStation. Ashly sometimes can't sleep, can you Ashly?

(Ashly shakes her head.)

Tutor: That must be hard for all of you. But what we are here to discuss are Ashly's GCSE options. She is finding combined science hard, aren't you Ashly? We have discussed her dropping it and replacing it with double science.

(Ashly looks at the floor and says nothing.)

Dad (angrily):   Ashly discussed all her GCSE options with us. These are the GCSEs she must take so that she can study medicine which has always been her dream. I cannot believe that you have discussed this with her without talking to us first. We chose this school because we knew it had such a good science department. Perhaps we have made the wrong choice. We will be discussing all of this further with your headteacher. We are going home now Ashly, come on.

The parents and Ashly leave the room.

So, what went wrong? How did the conversation move from concerned tutor to the parents threatening to remove their daughter from the school?

The next part of this chapter will explore what could have been done differently, by looking at how to create trust and emotional safety, rebalance the power dynamic, align stories, and avoid language traps.

Creating trust and emotional safety

Trust

Establishing mutual trust is key to the effectiveness of conversation. (If you don't know this by now, you probably haven't read the previous chapters.) Without establishing trust, difficult conversations become disagreements or arguments. In all other areas of life, developing trust takes time, sometimes years. In difficult conversations, we often only have minutes, but sometimes that's all it takes.

We form long-lasting impressions of people within the first few seconds of meeting them (Gladwell, 2005). The same is true of difficult conversations. In the first few moments of any interaction, our adaptive unconscious springs to life and judges whether we should feel safe or threatened. Those first few seconds are crucial in building the foundations of trust.

To create trust everyone must believe that their interests are kept in mind, their opinions respected, their motives are good (Patterson et al., 2012), and that they are valued. The tutor above thanks the parents for coming but does not acknowledge that it might have been hard for them to leave work in the middle of the day (**message: my job/role is more important than yours**). She introduces herself but does not give them time to introduce themselves (**message: I am more important than you**). In those first few sentences the parents have been made to feel unimportant and undervalued (**message from their brain: you are under threat**). Instead of creating trust, this will build defensiveness and anxiety. Ashly's presence is not really acknowledged at all (**message: your views don't count**).

Activity

Think of different ways in which the tutor could have greeted the parents and Ashly so that a trusting relationship could begin to develop from the first moments of the conversation

Emotional safety

In the first case study in this book a surgeon has to explain difficult options to parents who are struggling to deal with their son's pain. The feedback from the parents afterwards was that they felt they could trust the surgeon because she had taken time to talk with and listen to them. In fact, the whole conversation had lasted less than ten minutes. But by sitting with the parents, acknowledging and containing their worries, and responding with calm, concise clarity and certainty, she made them feel emotionally safe.

All conversations, difficult or easy, need to be underpinned by this feeling of emotional safety. Without emotional safety we will feel under threat and will not be able to hear or process what is being said or communicated to us; the whole conversation will be a waste of time.

In order to establish emotional safety, all those involved in a conversation must feel accepted (Whalley-Hammell, 2014), the purpose of the conversation must be agreed, there must be clear, shared expectations (Quiros et al., 2012), and everyone must feel that they have a stake in the outcome. At the beginning of the meeting, the tutor explains what her understanding of the purpose is but does not ask the parents or Ashly what they believe it to be (**message: you have no stake in this conversation; consequence: sense of threat**). The parents and Ashly are not given the chance to explain their hopes and expectations (**message: your views are not important; consequence: sense of lack of control and stake in outcome**).

Activity

List five things the tutor could have done to create a sense of emotional safety.

Rebalancing the power dynamic

As professionals we are often perceived as being in a position of authority, possessing the power to make important decisions about children, families, or patients. But if one person is perceived to hold all the power in a conversation, participants will feel that they have no control, influence, or power over the outcomes and will disengage or become resistant and defensive (Patterson et al., 2012). The philosopher Bertrand Russell (2004) believed that all social interactions are to some extent about power. This is also true in difficult conversations, where ensuring that power/control is equally distributed, and everyone believes their views hold equal value, is crucial if agreement is to be reached. Before the conversation begins it is a good idea to make a list (either mentally or physically) of who has what power. The results are often not what you would expect.

In the case study above the power distribution looks like this:

Table 4.1 Power distribution

Tutor	Parents	Ashly
Power/control over what support Ashly can be offered at school	Power/control over Ashly's Emotions (guilt and shame)	
	Power to agree/refuse Ashly dropping one subject for GCSE	
	Power to remove Ashly from school	

Whilst the parents perceive the tutor to have all the power, the above table shows that the true power lies with the parents. Most striking is Ashly who appears to have no power in a conversation that is about her. While we cannot change who has the power in the situation, we can change the power dynamics within the conversation so that everyone has a voice. To do this we need to consider the concept of locus of control (Rotter, 1954). Rotter introduced the idea that the extent to which we believe we have control over our lives depends on whether we attribute what happens to us to our own actions (internal locus of control) or to the actions of others (external locus of control) (Spector, 1988). Those with an external locus of control believe that there is no point in saying or doing anything because what happens to them is decided by the views and actions of others. (In this conversation, Ashly probably feels that her locus of control is completely external.) Conversely, those with an internal locus of control believe that what happens to them is dependent on their own decisions and actions. Professionally the tutor has an internal locus of control, but as the table shows, she has almost no control over decisions made about Ashly. To alter the power dynamic of the situation, the locus of control for each person must be moved. Everyone in the conversation must believe that there is a point to what they are saying and doing, that their actions will impact the outcome. Locus of control is both contextual and situational. There are things in our lives that we feel we have control over: the clothes we wear, what we have for lunch, how we get to work. But there are other things over which we feel we have very little control: decisions made by governments, wars, natural disasters. Just as our locus of control in life changes depending on the situation, so the locus of control in a difficult conversation can be altered. If this happens, power can be redistributed.

In the conversation above, the tutor takes immediate control of the situation, thanking parents for coming and setting the agenda (**message: I hold the power**

in this conversation). It is the tutor, not Ashly, who explains how Ashly is feeling (**message: I know Ashly better than anyone**). This belief that we know others better than they know themselves or us is called the 'Illusion of asymmetric insight' and can play a large part in unbalancing the power in a conversation as everyone tussles with each other to prove that their insight is greater.

It is Ashly's dad who describes how hard she is working and tells everyone what she wants to be (**message: I have control of what happens in my family**); it is the mum who provides context, about Ashly's current sleeping arrangement because of the grandmother's operation (**message: these things are difficult, but they are beyond my control**). Ashly's silence reflects an external locus of control (**message: there is no point in me saying anything because everyone else is deciding what happens to me**).

To change the subconscious messages, the power dynamic must be altered right from the beginning of the conversation. Every difficult conversation should begin by allowing everyone to speak, giving them the opportunity to explain what they are hoping to get out of the conversation. It must be made clear that no conclusion will be reached until everyone's views have been heard, explored, and understood, and there must always be time at the end of the conversation to summarise what has been agreed and clarify that there has been no misinterpretation. When a trusting relationship and emotional safety have been created, even those who usually have an external locus of control will feel able to speak and the power dynamic begins to shift.

Activity

Think of a difficult meeting you have had. Create a power distribution table (like Table 4.1). Under each name, write down one thing you could have done to create a more equal distribution of power.

Aligning stories

One of the things that makes difficult conversations so challenging is that we all approach them from a different angle, with contradictory interpretations. We might all be talking about the same person, the same event, the same problem, but our perception of what happened and of the consequences can be completely different. In Chapter 3, my son believed that I never listened to him, whilst I believed that I listened to him all the time. In the same way, when I was running a busy children's centre, the decision was made that we would take over the management of a smaller centre. Whilst I could see the potential for growth and partnership, members of both teams felt they would lose their role and identity; same story, different perceptions. Opposing stories such as these are what make conversations difficult. In the scenario above, Ashly is feeling overwhelmed by her workload, her dad believes that hard work is needed to succeed, her mum is worrying that Ashly is not getting enough sleep, and the tutor is concerned for Ashly's mental health. Same problem, four different stories. For a solution to be possible, these stories need to be aligned, creating what Patterson et al. (2012) call a shared pool of meaning that will allow shared solutions to emerge. What is important to remember is that all the views are of equal importance and that, despite seeming to contradict each other, they can all be true at the same time.

If there is trust and emotional safety, everyone should be able to add their views to the shared pool without fear of being judged and with the certainty that each story will be valued equally.

From the stories above, we have learnt that:

- Ashly's tutor is worried about her
- Ashly is feeling overwhelmed
- Ashly might be sleep-deprived because she is sleeping on the floor in her brother's room
- Ashly's mum is probably tired because she is looking after Ashly's grandmother
- Ashly is being compared to her brother who worked hard and got good grades
- Ashly's dad believes that hard work is what matters
- Ashly's dad wants her to become a doctor

All these stories are true. The trick is to find what they have in common and to check that no one's story is missing. The biggest problem here is that Ashly's story is absent. It is important that her story is told, perhaps with the support of her tutor if she lacks the confidence to speak, because any solution must include everyone's stories if a way forward is to be found. At the moment the conversation seems to be about Ashly without Ashly. Difficult conversations are not about who is right or who is wrong; nor are they about which facts are true and which are false – everyone believes their stories are true. Instead they are about unravelling 'conflicting perceptions, interpretations and values'

(Stone et al., 2023: 22) about gaining an understanding of what is important and about creating a new shared story, leading to the emergence of a shared solution. This can only happen when everyone has a stake in the outcome because everyone's story has been included as part of the process (Stone et al., 2023). In difficult conversations, individual stories can highlight unexpected problems. Be careful not to try and deal with all of them at the same time. Stay focused on the current issue and explore other problems in a future conversation. For example, it is not clear that Ashly wants to become a doctor; it seems that she is being measured against her brother. Although these are important problems, they are not the focus of the current conversation. Don't get sidetracked; align the stories around the current problem: what would help the parents to listen to Ashly's wish to drop a GCSE? If the dad understands that dropping one GCSE will not lessen Ashly's chances of applying for medical school and if her mum understands that this is likely to mean that Ashly is less tired, perhaps everyone's stories can be aligned, and a shared solution can be reached.

Activity

List three things the tutor could have done to ensure that everyone in the conversation feels that their voice has been heard. Consider what needs to be said or heard to bring the conversation to a shared solution.

Avoiding language traps

The final point to consider in this scenario is the language used – both spoken and unspoken. In previous chapters we have discussed the importance of body language, of facial expressions and gestures, of tone and intent. We have highlighted how silence and what is not said can be as important as what is said. The tutor makes a fatal error right at the beginning of this conversation by saying that she has a 'few concerns' about Ashly. This could be perceived as implying that: Ashly is not doing well academically, Ashly is ill, Ashly's behavior has not been good, her parents are to blame for whatever the problem is. Perhaps none of this is true, but what is heard in any conversation is more important than what is said, and what is understood is more important than what is meant (Ramsey, 2005). Reflecting on the language we use before we speak is crucial if we are to avoid misunderstandings (Fisher & Ury, 2011). Considering carefully what we are going to say and how we are going to say it can make or break a conversation, but there are some language 'tricks' that we can use to help and language 'traps' that we need to avoid.

Conversation tricks

Use 'and' instead of 'but' (Stone et al., 2023) – this avoids conversations becoming polarised. Using 'and' gives the message that everyone's views are equally valid. For example:

Tutor: Mr and Mrs Ryan, you want Ashly to get good grades in her exams and Ashly thinks this is more likely if she is studying one fewer GCSE.

By using 'and' instead of 'but', opposing concepts and ideas can become shared concepts (Fisher & Ury, 2011).

Focus on the problem, not the people

In difficult conversations, people often feel personally threatened, even if the focus of the conversation is a problem that has nothing to do with them. In the above scenario, Ashly's dad seems to have taken the fact that the tutor implied there was a concern about Ashly as a personal insult, whilst her mum seems to feel guilty.

Listen to all views with respect and courtesy and then refocus the conversation on the problem. Here is a possible way the tutor could have framed the issues:

Tutor to dad: I can hear how important your daughter's education is to you and how much you want to support her. Let's explore how we can work together to help Ashly reach her potential.

Tutor to mum: It must be exhausting having to look after your mum and all the family and it sounds like you are really trying to support Ashly with her work as well. What might make that easier?

Remember that acknowledging is not the same as agreeing

We can understand perfectly what someone is saying and disagree with it completely (Fisher & Ury, 2011). What is important is that everyone feels safe enough to be honest and tell their story. Consider the following:

Tutor responding to the dad:	You think these are the right GCSEs to ensure that Ashly can eventually apply for medical school.
Tutor responding to the mum:	You are worried that Ashly might not be getting enough sleep.
Tutor responding to Ashly:	You feel that you are studying too many GCSEs and are worried that you might fail.

Make it about you, not them

If you begin the conversation by talking about yourself, you demonstrate a willingness to make yourself vulnerable, opening the platform for honesty and preventing others from feeling threatened or under attack (Stone et al., 2023). Here is an example:

Tutor: As Ashly's tutor, it's my job to make sure that everything is going OK and that you and Ashly are happy with her progress and her choices. I always worry that I might have missed something. It's so good to have the chance to catch up with all of you.

Reflecting back, paraphrasing, and summarising

At the end of each part of a conversation, check that you have understood correctly by summarising and rewording what has been said. This shows that everyone has been heard. In the scenario, the tutor could have said:

Tutor: It sounds like there is a lot going on at home at the moment and that Ashly is working really hard.

What happens if they don't like me?

As stated earlier in this chapter, entering a conversation with a desire to be liked (Stone et al., 2023) leads to constant reassessment of how others perceive us rather than active listening and full participation in the discussion.

It is not about who is right and who is wrong

Difficult conversations are often the result of polarised thinking where everyone believes that their views are the only views, their way the only way, and that this is their chance to prove that they are right (Stone et al., 2023). It is always hard to accept that opposing views have equal validity to yours; but without this open-mindedness, difficult conversations will fail. What matters is gaining a better understanding of everyone's viewpoint and using this knowledge to build bridges.

Avoid the blame game

Blaming others for what has happened will always be counterproductive. People who are being blamed feel as though they are under attack and will respond by becoming defensive or angry. Either way they will stop listening to what is being said and are very likely to fight back (Fisher & Ury, 2011). This will not lead to resolution but to arguments and a breakdown in communication (Stone et al, 2005).

Avoid disguising statements as questions

It is easy to fall into the trap of making a point by asking a question:

'Are you going to finish the washing up before you go to bed?' when what we mean is:
  'Please could you do the washing up?'

By questioning we force people into a corner, often because it shames them or makes them feel guilty. It can lead to resentment and defensiveness, but rarely leads to a solution or the dishes being washed before bedtime. Honesty and transparency will always create better solutions than hiding what you really mean in a question (Stone et al., 2023).

Reframing the conversation

Finally, let's revisit the scenario above using some of the ideas explored in this chapter.

Environment: the head of the school has let the meeting take place in her office where there will be no noise from pupils going home and where there is a round table where everyone can sit. The tutor offers everyone tea and coffee before the conversation begins.

The conversation re-imagined

Tutor: Mr and Mrs Ryan, my name is Emily Greenrow and I am Ashly's tutor. First of all, I wanted to thank you for coming. I know how hard it is to take time off in the middle of the day.

As Ashly's tutor, it's my job to make sure that everything is going OK and that you and Ashly are happy with her progress and her choices. I always worry that I might have missed something. It's so good to have the chance to catch up with all of you and I hope that everyone will find this discussion useful.

Mum and Dad: Thank you.

Tutor: Before we start, shall we go round the table and find out what everyone would like to talk about? Mr Ryan, would you like to start?

Dad: I would like to know how well Ashly is doing and what she will need to do to make sure she gets into medical school when she leaves school. We chose this school because we know it has a good reputation for science.

Tutor: Thank you. Can I just check that I have written this down correctly: you want to check on Ashly's progress and to find out more about applying for medical school.

Dad: That's right.

Tutor: Mrs Ryan, is there anything in particular you would like to talk about?

Mum: I just want to make sure that Ashly is not too tired at school. Her grandma has had a hip replacement and is staying at our house while she recovers. She is in Ashly's room, so Ashly is sleeping on a mattress in her brother's room. I hope that her work is not suffering because of this.

Tutor: It must be hard for you looking after your mother as well as everyone else. I hope you are getting enough rest too! Thank you for telling me; it's always so helpful to know if something has changed at home. So, you just want to check that Ashly is doing OK at school and that her work is not suffering. I have that written down. Ashly and I met the

55

other day and there is something she is worried about. We wrote it down. Ashly did you want to read it out or would you like me to explain what we talked about?

(Ashly takes the piece of paper without looking at her mum and dad.)

Ashly: I really want to get the best grades in my GCSEs but doing combined science with all my other GCSEs is a lot of work and I am worried that I won't get such good grades if I carry on. I would like to take double science instead. I think it would really help.

Dad: But your brother did combined science and he managed to get very good grades. And what about medical school? How will you get in if you drop a GCSE?

(Ashly looks down at the table.)

Tutor: You are right, Mr Ryan, academic skills are important for getting into university, but other things are important too. Things have changed since Ashly's brother did his GCSEs. Ashly is doing very well academically but she is also volunteering in our library once a week over lunchtime, helping on our peer reading scheme, and she is on the hockey team.

Dad: How does this help with her exam results? She needs to give these things up and focus on her studies so she can get into a good university.

Tutor: Universities today prioritise students who do well academically *and* have been involved in extracurricular activities. We checked and if Ashly does want to apply for medical school, double science will be enough, especially with all the other things she does. The peer reading tutors speak so highly of Ashly and all that she does to help. You should both be very proud of her.

(Mum and dad smile.)

Mum: Ashly, do you think if you drop this one GCSE, you will feel less stressed and tired?

(Ashly nods.)

(Mum looks at dad. He sighs.)

Dad:	Ashly, if this what you want, I will agree but you must work very hard on your studies You must promise not to spend all your time doing other things.
Ashly (quietly):	I promise.
Dad:	OK. We agree to you dropping just this GCSE. Tutor, please can we arrange another meeting like this next term so we can check that Ashly's progress continues and that she is not doing too many of the extracurricular activities. Next meeting you might need to drop one of these, Ashly.

(Ashly nods.)

Tutor:	Of course. I think that is an excellent idea. I am so glad that you think this has been useful. I wish that all parents thought the same way as you! Before you go, can I just check that I have remembered everything right: it has been agreed that Ashly can drop a GCSE and that she can continue with all her extracurricular activities for now but that we will review this next time we meet?
Mum and Dad:	Yes, that is right.
Tutor:	Great. Thank you again for coming in. Please ask the school secretary to make a date for that meeting on the way out. Ashly, are you OK with all of this?
Ashly:	Yes, thank you. I feel much better now.

The family leave the room together.

Conclusion

Difficult conversations do not come with an instruction booklet; there are no one-size-fits-all solutions because there are no one-size-fits-all conversations. Being part of a difficult conversation can feel daunting and challenging, but using strategies, concepts, and ideas like those explored in this chapter can help to move a conversation from difficult to effective, from polarised to shared, from conflict to resolution.

Key takeaways

- Stay calm when emotions are exploding around you
- Do not try to make people like you
- Remember it is not about who is right or who is wrong; it is about trying to understand each other's stories
- Acknowledging the views of others is not the same as agreeing with them
- Always think about the power dynamic

References

Barsade, S.G., Coutifaris, C.G., &Pillemer, J. (2018). Emotional contagion in organizational life. *Research in Organizational Behavior, 38*, 137–151.

Dunbar, R.I.M. (1996). *Grooming, gossip, and the evolution of language*. Cambridge, MA: Harvard University Press.

Fisher, R., & Ury, W., with Patton, B. (Ed.) (2011). *Getting to YES* (3rd ed.). London: Penguin.

Gladwell, M. (2005). *BLINK: The power of thinking without thinking*. London: Penguin.

Patterson, K., Grenny, J., McMillan, R., & Switzler, A. (2012). *Crucial conversations: Tools for talking when stakes are high*. New York: McGraw-Hill Education.

Pickering, M.J., & Garrod, S. (2004). Toward a mechanistic psychology of dialogue. *Behavioral and Brain Sciences, 27*(2), 169–190.

Quiros, L., Kay, L., & Montijo, A. (2012). Creating emotional safety in the classroom and in the field. *Reflections: Narratives of Professional Helping, 18*(2), 42–47.

Ramsey, R. (2005). *Lead, follow, or get out of the way: How to be a more effective leader in today's schools*. Thousand Oaks, CA: Corwin Press.

Rotter, J. (1954). *Social learning and clinical psychology*. Englewood Cliffs, NJ: Prentice-Hall.

Russell, B. (2004). *Power: A new social analysis*. London: Routledge Classics.

Spector, P.E. (1988). Development of the Work Locus of Control Scale. *Journal of Occupational Psychology, 61*, 335–340.

Stone, D., Patton, B., & Heen, S. (2023). *Difficult conversations: How to discuss what matters most*. London: Penguin.

Whalley-Hammell, K. (2014). Belonging, occupation, and human well-being: An exploration. *Canadian Journal of Occupational Therapy, 81*(1), 39–50.

Part 2

Why does it all go wrong – again and again... and again?

5

Monkeys with smartphones? When our emotions take control

Introduction

Have you ever said something 'in the heat of the moment' that you do not really mean? Alternatively, have you said something you do mean, but later wish you had not said it? We have all probably had the experience of opening our mouths and leaving bruised feelings, or worse, in our wake. Then again, there are surely few of us who have not gone into a difficult meeting, with absolute clarity about what we are going to say, only for our minds to go blank; or, we managed to find the right words; it was just a shame that they did not come out in the right order. This can be very frustrating, not least because in the professions we follow we are supposed to be skilled communicators. Equally frustrating, and potentially undermining, can be those situations we approach with an expectation that we are going to make a mess of things, because when we are nervous, we usually do. Why, we might ask, do our wonderfully tuned, professionally schooled brains seem to let us down, just when we need them most?

Of course, this may not be your experience at all; you may manage all difficult and adversarial communication in a calm and collected manner. You may even relish these moments of challenge, emerging invigorated and validated by a job well done. If this is the case, you can either skip this chapter or read it and wonder why other people find these things so difficult. Alternatively, you may see whether the following pages have anything of resonance for you, because we will be exploring the basics of human nature; how our brains work and why they become befuddled; why we do and say things that we may later regret; and why we always think of the clever retort or put-down *after* we have left the room.

Why monkeys with smartphones?

The title of this chapter is 'Monkeys with Smartphones?' Its basic premise is that all human beings are navigating the complexities of modern life with

DOI: 10.4324/9781003433248-7

brains that were designed for a completely different set of challenges. In essence, brains that evolved to deal with the very real threat of predators and other forms of physical danger are not sufficiently attuned to deal with the lower-level, but frequent or continuous stressors of modern life. A suitable analogy is that of imagining our brains as an ancient computer trying to run the latest Windows or iOS programs (modern life). It may not be a particularly good analogy: I know little about computers, other than my ability to switch them on and shout at them when they go wrong. Any psychologists or neuroscientists who happen to be reading may have concluded that I know even less about the brain, because it is far more complicated than I have described. Therefore, I should stress that I am *not* a psychologist, nor a neuroscientist. In my view, I do not need to be. My aim, over the next few pages, is to focus on the impact of how we *experience* how our brains work, rather than delve too deeply into the complexities of neurological structures and processes. The material I have included has helped me understand how and why I react the way I do in certain situations: I hope you will find it useful, too.

Case study: Erica

Erica is a capable and conscientious worker. She is highly intelligent, empathetic, and caring. Similarly, Erica is logical and a very good problem solver, and her colleagues respect her decision-making abilities and her ability to stay calm in a crisis. What they do not know is that Erica always feels that she struggles to get her point across in highly emotional or conflictual situations; she feels her head starting to freeze and finds that she cannot find the words she needs. She dreads certain meetings and having to speak to certain people. She fears that she will come over as flustered, unprofessional, and nervous. This chapter has been written for the Ericas and Erics of this world.

Not evolved enough?

At this point, early in the chapter, I run the risk of contradicting myself. Throughout human evolution, the brain has of course evolved; it is not a ZX Spectrum or an early model Apple Mac, their capabilities frozen in time by the limits of their processing chips. In the course of human history, the brain has tripled in size (Holloway, 1996) and with this has come an increase in complexity, processing power, and the ability to do the things we think of as being inherently human: language, creativity, and reasoning are but a few (DeFelipe, 2011). In addition, it is important to remember that cognitive ability is not merely a function of brain size (De Felipe, 2011; DeCasien et al., 2022); rather, certain structures of the brain have evolved in their sophistication and in their consequent ability to perform the functions we commonly associate with human consciousness. Key among these are the activities that we might loosely term 'thinking': the ability to produce ideas, make decisions, problem-solve, imagine, and remember (VandenBos, 2007). However, particularly in times of stress, there can be a disconnection between what we might like to believe about our ability to be calm, thoughtful, and rational and our actual experience of being hostage to our emotions, fears, and anxieties. Later in the chapter we will explore in more detail what happens when our emotions 'take over' in difficult conversations, but at this point let us consider that the higher cognitive functions that we associate with being human emerged relatively late in our evolutionary story (Roth & Dicke, 2019). Many structures, processes, and functions found in the brains we all possess are far more ancient and not as sophisticated (Le Doux, 2019) as we would like to believe. It is these, less evolved, structures that can dominate when we are under stress, often seeming to overwhelm and even sabotage our best intentions when engaging in difficult discussions.

The better safe than sorry principle

The primary purpose of the brain is to keep us alive. It is not that its other purposes are not important; it is just that if the brain fails to keep us alive, everything else is a little redundant. The brain keeps us alive through delivering and managing our physiological functions, but also, critically, through being obsessively focused on keeping us safe (Van der Kolk, 2014). Researchers have argued that structures and processes that the brain deploys to keep us safe developed earlier on in our evolutionary history than those associated with our higher cognitive functions (MacLean, 1990; Van der Kolk, 2014). As such, they lack a degree of nuance and sophistication, which makes them overreact to the everyday stresses and anxieties of modern life. I have found it helpful to understand our brains' safety mechanisms in terms of the 'precautionary principle': in short, they work to the adage of 'better safe than sorry'. If you want to see this principle in action, you might see how your pet reacts to a sudden disturbance or loud noise. Typically, they will run away, which is one of the cluster of responses we know as 'fight, flight, freeze'.

Your pet's brain does not care whether the disturbance, for example a loud noise, is something that may be harmful or merely a car backfiring on the road outside; it does not wait long enough to find out – the pet is automatically employing the 'better safe than sorry' principle. For our early ancestors this worked well; being hypervigilant and overreacting at the first sign of possible danger kept them alive. Running away or hiding, or even getting ready to fight, when they detected a rustle in the bushes, meant that our early ancestors probably had a stressful time on a windy day, but, if the bushes had turned out to be hiding a lion, at least they did not get eaten.

Activity

Read back through the case study about Erica. How does her response in meetings link to the 'better safe than sorry' principle?

Unconscious reactions

You may be wondering what lions, bushes, and hypervigilance have to do with communication. The key point is that our brains still operate on the 'better safe than sorry' principle, with a tendency to overreact to things that the brain quickly and unconsciously decides may harm us. The brain does not care whether they are actually harmful or not; its first job is to keep us safe. Later in the chapter, we will have a look at these safety mechanisms and how they may impact both on our perception and on our communication, but at this stage it is useful to consider that the structures and processes that detect and respond to threat are in many ways not as sophisticated as those that deal with those complicated, beautiful 'human' skills that we all know, love, and need. MacLean (1990) provided a way of understanding this with his model of the 'triune' brain, triune literally meaning 'three in one'. MacLean suggested that the brain could be subdivided into three 'layers', each of which had its origins in different phases of our evolutionary history. The oldest division of the brain MacLean called the 'reptilian brain', which deals with physiological functions. The 'mammalian brain' is situated on top of the reptilian brain and supports and sustains our emotional life. Critically, in the context of this chapter the mammalian brain contains two structures, the amygdala and hypothalamus, which enable us to detect and respond to danger. However, this system is not sufficiently refined to identify nuance when it comes to threat; it works on the better safe than sorry principle, but also – crucially – initiates relatively unsubtle responses to perceived danger: anger, aggression, fear, mentally and physically freezing; a desire to escape (LeDoux, 2019). These take place automatically, often before we are aware that they are *taking place*. They are also not hugely responsive to our own conscious intervention; we can tell ourselves not to run away; but next time you are feeling nervous, tell yourself not to and see how that works out.

The battle for control: Unconscious vs conscious reactions

Our conscious efforts to regulate our emotions come under the heading of 'top-down control'. Top-down refers to the final division and most recent addition to the triune brain, the *neocortex* or *primate brain* and specifically the *prefrontal cortex* behind our foreheads. Although the various structures in the brain are highly interconnected, the prefrontal cortex has limited ability to modify our emotional responses under conditions of high stress (Van der Kolk, 2014). The primate brain may have the subtlety and finesse to correctly appraise potential danger and harm. However, if the less sophisticated structures in the brain are sounding a very loud fire alarm, the brain will operate on, you guessed it, the better safe than sorry principle.

It should be noted that, even when first published, the triune brain theory was contested by many neuroscientists as being too simplistic or downright inaccurate. However, it provides a useful means of understanding how and why we may behave as we do. Another analogous model was proposed by Professor Steve Peters in 2012. In *The Chimp Paradox*, Peters proposes that the prefrontal cortex, or as he terms it the *human brain*, exists in a struggle for control with our *chimp brain* or limbic system (the mammalian brain in MacLean's triune brain theory). Peters' model suggests that the human condition is essentially a clash between rationality and emotion. However, let us now turn to the work of Daniel Kahneman, who delved deeper into the manner in which human beings *think*.

Thinking about thinking

Arguably, when we think about thinking we focus on *conscious* thought. However, Daniel Kahneman revolutionised the way we understand thinking. His Nobel Prize-winning research was summarised in his best-selling book *Thinking, Fast and Slow* (Kahneman, 2011). Kahneman suggested that the brain creates thoughts in two different ways, which he characterised as System 1 and System 2 thinking.

System 1 thinking is fast, unconscious, and processes information based on prior experience; in essence the brain looks for patterns based on what it already knows and appraises situations accordingly. When applied to communication, we appraise what we anticipate someone might say based on our experience of them or similar social interactions. This is a wonderful skill; we might imagine how strange life would be if, every time someone smiled and said 'hello' to us, we had to work out what to do next. However, there is a cost to this relatively effortless, quick, and smooth way of thinking. System 1 thinking is quick because it takes mental shortcuts. It makes sense of the world in terms of our past experience, and with that comes the biases and prejudices that we may not be consciously aware of. Consequently, System 1 thinking is quick to jump to conclusions: sometimes when looking for patterns from which to make sense of a situation, it can join the dots and form the wrong picture.

Activity

If you sense that your emotions are in control, perhaps when you are feeling highly anxious or worried, take two deep breaths – breathing in for a count of 7 and out for a count of 11. This will slow down your heart rate, bring oxygen back to your brain and help you to access your System 2 thinking.

Transference

Unfortunately, because System 1 thinking is unconscious, we may not be aware that the reason we feel irritated with someone is because the unconscious brain has concluded that they look a bit like our mother, or they sound like the schoolteacher we hated when we were 14. And, of course, here is another problem – you may also remind another person of their irritating parent, spouse, teacher, or dentist.

Those with a counselling or similar therapeutic knowledge might recognise in the last paragraph some similarities with the concepts of *transference*, defined as 'the displacement of an emotion or attitude from one person to another person' (Tudor & Merry, 2006: 143). For example, someone might remind you of a parent, friend, or sibling and, without realising it, you start reacting to and communicating with them, as if they were that parent, friend, sibling, or colleague. Within the therapeutic professions there is a distinction made between transference and *countertransference*: transference being the projection of the client's feelings towards the therapist and countertransference being projection in the other direction. An example often given in the counselling literature is where a practitioner may feel protective towards a client because the client displays vulnerabilities that remind the therapist of their own child (Racker, 2018).

Case study: James

James has recently begun working in a service supporting young people. James has found that one of the young people, Molly, seems to irritate him, but he is also quite protective of her. When he is supposed to challenge Molly about some of the things she has been doing, he finds that he avoids asking difficult questions. When Molly gets angry or distressed, James finds that he feels guilty and frequently ends up doing things for Molly that she could be doing for herself. Molly is a similar age to James' teenage daughter who left home following a family argument and from whom James is estranged.

What is going on with James?

James seems to be transferring emotions linked to his relationship with his daughter onto Molly. There are many suggested ways of dealing with transference and countertransference (Racker, 2018). However, the first step is recognition; this can be achieved through supervision for James and through self-awareness and reflection. It is beyond the scope of this book to explore too deeply the theme of reflective practice; readers will probably have experience of the concept or may wish to consult the many books or journal articles on the subject. However, a useful place to start is being aware of our own history, the anxieties we have about people and the needs we have from them. It could be that we like to be liked or have a need to be needed, or, if we have been let down by people in the past, we might project the feelings about those people into the present. In this case study, James is transferring all his emotions for his estranged daughter onto Molly: feeling irritated with her because his last conversation with his daughter was an argument, feeling guilty when she gets upset because he hasn't managed to patch things up with his daughter, feeling protective because, as a dad, he wants to make sure his daughter is safe, doing things for her because he can't do them for his daughter. This can impact on our communication and our ability to engage with honesty. It can lead to confusing conversations for those in receipt of unexpected emotional responses, in this case, Molly. James might also want Molly to like him. Needing to be liked may result in failure to be assertive or avoiding difficult conversations. A need to be needed may result in us, subconsciously, keeping people dependent on us or being reluctant to recognise if others' expectations of us are unrealistic or unhealthy – here James has let Molly become dependent on him for things she could do herself. If we have been hurt, we may be hypervigilant to being hurt again and see in others the warning signs that we missed before. Remember that the safety features of the brain cannot process and do not care whether the *potential* harm is real; 'better safe than sorry' is the order of the day. So, James might overcompensate in his relationship with Molly, just in case she hurts him the way his daughter has hurt him.

This is why it is useful to engage all that fancy neural circuitry in the neocortex, which has the tools to more accurately recognise what is going on for us. Once recognised, setting and maintaining professional boundaries can be critical; again, there are a range of works that explore this. One useful tip is to identify exactly what it is that reminds us of another person in the person we are working with, then actively contemplate the differences between them (Oelsner, 2013). James needs to do this in order to respond to Molly as a client, rather than as his daughter. Empathy, or the ability to attempt to see the world through another's eyes, is especially useful, particularly if you have some idea of the other person's history. As a social worker I spent a great deal of my career rushing from one visit to the next, arriving in a screech of burning rubber (I always seemed to be late) and catapulting myself into people's lives without having thought through what I was going to do when I got there. I would rely on my mouth eventually catching up with my brain, or vice versa, after about five minutes or so. I was lucky enough to encounter a technique known as 'tuning in' (Cournoyer, 2016) where, no matter how pressed for time, I spent a minute or so trying to put myself in the shoes of the person or people I was meeting. Key questions were: What might the person be expecting from me? How might they react to me? What might be their assumptions, prejudices, or anxieties? Tuning in is explored further in the chapter on relationships.

These techniques are characteristic of what Kahneman (2011) termed System 2 thinking, which is slow, conscious, analytical, requires effort, and, because it requires energy, can be tiring. We may like to think that we are rational, analytical, careful, and deliberate. However, Kahneman suggests that it is in fact System 1 thinking that is the dominant partner with System 2 being brought into action when we make an effort to employ it, or when we encounter something that System 1 needs help dealing with. It should be noted that the two systems don't operate in isolation, but we should recognise that we spend most of our day dealing with people and the rest of the world through habitual mechanisms that are based on what we already know and are heavily influenced by our emotions. Often, when we are particularly stressed, we may find it difficult to access System 2 thinking, we may experience 'brain fog', indecisiveness, and an inability to string a coherent sentence together. For James, the rift between himself and his daughter has left him feeling emotionally raw. He feels constantly guilty and is forever watching out for her return. He might tell himself that Molly is not his daughter, but his brain makes him respond as though she is, just in case. So let us now turn to these mysterious things called emotions – why we need them and what their influence is on communication. We may characterise this state in ourselves and others as being 'over-emotional'.

Activity

Think about a time you were surprised by your own emotional response to someone. Can you link this back to transference? Were you actually responding to someone else?

What are emotions?

The term 'over-emotional', which I have just used, shows that emotions can get a bit of bad press. Yes, they may be all about love and compassion, but also anger, jealousy, and suspicion. 'Letting your emotions get the better of you' is 'unprofessional', 'irrational', and potentially dangerous. Surely, the goal for any right-thinking professional is to be a model of impassive cool and rationality. It is just that humans do not work that way, and it is just as well that they do not.

Emotions are responses to chemical messages in our brains and bodies, neurotransmitters, or hormones. Neurotransmitters provide the chemical link in the gaps between neurons; they have a short response time, affect voluntary and involuntary actions, and fade away quickly (Webster, 2001). Hormones are released into our bloodstream from the endocrine glands, although some like melatonin and cortisol are produced in the brain. They are involuntary – we cannot mentally control our hormones – and are longer lasting than neurotransmitters (McEwen, 2020).

From at least the eighteenth century Western scientific and philosophical thought created a false distinction between rational thought and emotion. Philosophers and scientists, predominately male, sought to define 'modern', rational human beings against their 'emotional' forebears. Of course, it will no doubt come as a surprise to learn that they were also defining themselves against 'excitable' foreigners and 'hysterical' women. If we are very charitable, these attitudes may be considered old-fashioned at best. However, they still have a legacy in terms of how we think we should behave and feel. Being 'cool, calm, and collected' is an aspiration for many of us and a source of self-criticism, guilt, or shame if we do not meet that self-imposed standard. However, studies have indicated much of the cool rationality expressed at work is merely an attempt to suppress anxiety. Gabriel (1998) and Flam (2002) reveal how managers suppress, behind a mask of rational detachment, the anxiety and fear that arises from the uncertainties of their work. In the Erica case study, you will remember that she feared appearing flustered, unprofessional, and nervous.

We are not suggesting that our working lives should be underpinned by conspicuous displays of emotion, but that emotions are integral both to System 1 thinking and that number one duty of the brain – keeping us safe. Therefore, let us try and bring together all the elements we have discussed and return to the question posed in the introductory paragraphs: Why does our brain let us down just when we need it most? And how does this impact our ability to communicate successfully in difficult conversations?

When our emotions take control

Strictly speaking it is not our emotions that are taking control; they are merely manifestations of the automatic safety mechanisms that are triggered when our brains detect potential threats. We have discussed in previous chapters the way an imminent difficult conversation can fill us with a sense of dread. Remember that the brain does not know or care whether the threat is real; it does not wait to find out before initiating what have been termed automatic 'pre-programmed escape strategies' (Van der Kolk, 2014), which we might understand in terms of the *fight, flight, freeze* responses to danger. In my teaching, for the past 20 years, I have used the term 'inner meerkat' to describe how, even at rest, our brains are automatically and continually scanning for potential threats. As such, they resemble a meerkat standing on its hind legs constantly looking out for danger. It is a relatively simple concept to explain to both adults and children, although I was once asked by an eager 8-year-old what their inner meerkat ate and how often they should feed it.

Meerkats scatter at the first sign of trouble, and we start to react *before we are consciously aware of it* if our brains catch the first indication of potential danger. I promised that I would not take us on a neurological grand tour, but it is worth taking a few minutes discussing what happens inside our brains and bodies when our meerkat detects danger (and for this, we do not need to bring a bag of peanuts with us).

LeDoux (2019) suggests that information comes into our brain through our senses. These signals go up to the neocortex and our conscious awareness, what he calls 'the high road'. Simultaneously, 'the low road' takes these signals down to our limbic system, the emotion centres of the mammalian brain and particularly a small structure called the *amygdala*. Van der Kolk (2014) calls the amygdala the brain's smoke detector and, much as a smoke detector can set off the alarm in response to burnt toast and excessive showering, the amygdala similarly overreacts. Obviously, we do not run out of the door, roll into a ball, or shout at someone every time we get stressed – or at least I hope that is the case, tempting as it may be on some days. This is because our conscious brain, particularly the frontal cortex, or 'Watchtower' as termed by Van der Kolk, can work out that a stroppy email is not actually going to kill us. The trouble for us is that, to keep us safe, the information coming through our senses reaches the smoke detector before the watchtower – and we are already reacting to danger before we become consciously aware of it.

What does this mean for our communication? Part of our stress response involves the release of hormones called *glucocorticoids*. These flood the neocortex and result in the woolly thinking, brain freeze, and inability to string a sentence together, which Erica, in the case study, feared so much. Simultaneously, glucocorticoids stimulate the amygdala and prompt the retrieval of emotional memories of all the bad things that have happened to us in the past that are like the situation we are in in the present. We are not consciously aware of these emotional memories; we just get the bad feelings. Crucially, these make the situation seem worse than it is – they are meant to, as the brain wants us to avoid unpleasantness, just in case it might harm us, and really wants us to pay attention to any potential threat that it has detected, based on our past experience and emotional memories.

Activity

At the end of your working day, try to note down all the good things that have happened that day. (This is hard because, to stop us repeating mistakes, our brain focuses on the negative things that have happened.) This task can help our System 2 thinking override our System 1 thinking.

Avoid overthinking

This is an example of how the safety mechanisms in our brain have not evolved sufficiently to deal with the challenges of modern life. In the twenty-first century it is useful to be able to defend ourselves verbally – to process what other people are saying and be able to get our points across. The problem is that you do not debate a predator, and dealing with predators is what our brains evolved to do. In fact, 'overthinking' can be potentially dangerous; it's quicker to work on the 'better safe than sorry' principle. A further feature of our safety mechanisms is that, under stress, the brain's priorities become very short-term. This is why people say things that they do not mean, or at least regret, while having an argument. The brain's priority is to deal with the immediate threat; it is 'in the moment' and the future does not matter.

Activity

Before a difficult conversation, try going for a walk or moving around. This can 'use up' some of the adrenaline coursing through your body when you are experiencing a 'fight, flight, freeze' response and helps to regulate your breathing and your thinking so that you are mentally prepared.

What can be done?

Much as I would like you to believe that I am a paragon of tolerance, calm and witty repartee when under stress, sadly I am not. It was even more disappointing to realise, despite having read a lot of things, had a few 'Eureka' moments, and even having the chutzpah to think I can write something that helps other people, I too struggle with this stuff. Therefore, the next few paragraphs will discuss things that I know have been helpful for me, and for others. They may not all work for you.

Firstly, and returning to our friend Erica, there is little point berating ourselves for the way we are made. Our brain and, in this context, our emotional responses to things are shaped by our experiences (Van der Kolk, 2014). This means that some of us will be more affected by certain situations than our colleagues and friends. This is not a weakness, although it is perhaps human nature to focus on the things we do not like about ourselves rather than on the positives. It is also more than likely that there is a positive flip side to some of our personal characteristics that we find irritating. For example, someone who does not like conflict may be incredibly empathetic; their avoidance of conflict may be the result of feeling the hurt of others.

The second thing to remember is that System 1 thinking is very powerful and runs on patterns that can be quite hard to shift, not least because we are not always aware of them. We are creatures of habit, and habits can be very resistant to change. We may make promises to ourselves to be 'more X' or 'less y' in the future, but this can be difficult to achieve. We have covered why this might be in our discussion about how the brain functions under stress. What we have not discussed is that, when we are tired, ill, over-worked, hungry, or dehydrated, our ability to 'self-regulate' can be diminished (Heatherton, 2011). How many of us return from a Christmas break, full of New Year resolutions that do not seem to survive the first week of contact with work. This is normal and natural; it is not our fault.

Conclusion

Rest assured that at this point we are not going to suggest that each morning we look in the mirror, 'forgive ourselves', and recite some life-affirming message. This may work for some people, but we have both seen what we look like in the morning, and it is a profoundly disappointing experience.

Rather, we suggest working with and from who and what we are instead of what we think we should be. In their book *Crucial Conversations*, Patterson et al. (2002) suggest being honest with ourselves about how we typically react in stressful situations. Knowing this, we can at least plan for difficult encounters and conversations. Using some of the activities in this chapter we can develop strategies to do battle with our monkey brain and enable our System 2 thinking to guide our difficult conversations.

Key takeaways

- Employ the tuning in technique
- Make a difficult phone call standing up or pacing back and forth. This mimics the flight response
- Write down the key points you want to make before a conversation
- Stick to your points
- If you are initiating a conversation, rehearse your opening line

References

Cournoyer, B.R. (2016). *The social work skills workbook*. Boston, MA: Cengage Learning.

DeCasien, A.R., Barton, R.A., & Higham, J.P. (2022). Understanding the human brain: Insights from comparative biology. *Trends in Cognitive Sciences, 26*(5), 432–445.

DeFelipe, J. (2011). The evolution of the brain, the human nature of cortical circuits, and intellectual creativity. *Frontiers in neuroanatomy, 5*, 29.

Flam, H. (2002). Corporate emotions and emotions in corporations. In J. Barbalet (Ed.), *Emotions and sociology*. Oxford: Blackwell Publishing.

Gabriel, Y. (1998). Psychoanalytic Contributions to the study of the emotional life of corporations. *Administration and Society, 30*(3), 291–314.

Heatherton, T.F. (2011). Neuroscience of self and self-regulation. *Annual Review of Psychology, 62*(1), 363–390.

Holloway, R. (1996). Evolution of the human brain. In A. Lock & C.R. Peters (Eds.), *Handbook of human symbolic evolution*. Oxford: Oxford University Press.

Kahneman, D. (2011). *Thinking, fast and slow*. New York: Allen Lane.

LeDoux, J. (2019). *The deep history of ourselves: The four-billion-year story of how we got conscious brains*. New York: Viking.

MacLean, P.D. (1990). *The triune brain in evolution: Role in paleocerebral functions*. New York: Springer Science & Business Media.

McEwen, B.S. (2020). Hormones and behavior and the integration of brain-body science. *Hormones and Behavior, 119*, 104619.

Oelsner, R. (Ed.). (2013). *Transference and countertransference today*. London: Routledge.

Patterson, K., Grenny, J., McMillan, R., & Switzler, A. (2002). *Crucial conversations: Tools for talking when stakes are high*. New York: McGraw-Hill Education.

Peters, S. (2012). *The chimp paradox: The mind management program to help you achieve success, confidence, and happiness*. London: Vermillion.

Racker, H. (2018). *Transference and countertransference*. London: Routledge.

Roth, G., & Dicke, U. (2019). Origin and evolution of human cognition. *Progress in Brain Research, 250*, 285–316.

Tudor K., & Merry, T. (2006). *Dictionary of person-centred psychology*. Ross-on-Wye: PCCS Books.

VandenBos, G.R. (2007). *APA dictionary of psychology*. Washington, DC: American Psychological Association.

Van der Kolk, B. (2014). *The body keeps the score: Mind, brain and body in the transformation of trauma*. Harmondsworth: Penguin.

Webster, R. (Ed.). (2001). *Neurotransmitters, drugs and brain function*. Chichester: John Wiley & Sons.

6

It's all about relationships

Introduction: 'What is the matter with them? What have I done wrong?'

The basic premise of this book is that difficult conversations are usually conducted with another person or people. Of course, it is possible to have a difficult conversation with yourself, but that is probably a topic best left to moral philosophers and singer–songwriters; it is certainly outside the scope of this book. Few of us would likely disagree if I suggested that it is easy to be misunderstood. Similarly, it is likely that most of us will have had the experience of being in discussions where we think we are being completely reasonable, but the other person appears to be wilfully misunderstanding what we say, ascribing to us unfair motives that we do not have, or are verbally attacking before we have said anything at all.

Case study: Billy and Charlie

Billy has approached Charlie to discuss a possible pay rise. Billy has not previously discussed this with Charlie and thought it best to take a direct and spontaneous approach, rather than arrange a specific meeting. In fact, Billy had not really given the issue much attention until they had learned that someone in another department was being paid more for apparently doing less. Billy is feeling a bit aggrieved but is also quite nervous about broaching the subject. They have briefly rehearsed what they want to say. Conscious of their nervousness, Billy has deliberately opted for what they think is a serious, no-nonsense, and professional tone.

Billy: Charlie, I really need to talk to you about something important.
Charlie: What is the problem now?

           DOI: 10.4324/9781003433248-8

Billy: Nothing is a problem now, Charlie. I just wanted to talk about ... oh, it doesn't matter.

Charlie: But you said it was important; if there is a problem I need to know about it.

Billy: Really, there isn't a problem.

Charlie: But you have just come in here saying you needed to talk to me. Then you say there isn't a problem. What is it? I'm up to my ears here. I haven't got a lot of time, Billy!

Billy: Charlie, it does not matter. I shouldn't have bothered you. It ... is ... fine!

Billy leaves Charlie's office. Charlie is bewildered and irritated, wondering what they had done wrong and why Billy always seems so oversensitive: what is the matter with them!

Billy is seething about Charlie: What is the matter with them? What have I done wrong?

Activity

At this point, take a few seconds to review the dialogue. What do you think has gone wrong here?

It is probably the case that all of us have had the experience of conversations taking on an energy or momentum of their own. In the previous chapter we explored how human stress reactions can lead us to focus on the short term, inhibit our ability to think clearly, and make us quick to anger, or to overreact in other ways. If we focus on Charlie, we can reasonably conclude from the statement 'I am up to my ears' that they are stressed and beset by problems. They have misinterpreted Billy's 'I really need to talk to you about something important' and Billy's serious tone as indicating that there is another problem to be dealt with. As discussed in the last chapter, people often interpret and prejudge a new situation in terms of what they are currently dealing with, expect to be dealing with, and what they already know (Kahneman, 2011). This appears to be what Charlie is doing, perhaps adding a dose of impatience into the mix.

In our experience, when conversations start to unravel, there is often a pivot point that can act, often unwittingly, as a 'red rag to a bull'. In this instance, we would suggest that this occurs when Charlie says: 'what is the problem **now**?' Of course, we do not know Charlie's tone of voice, but if they are stressed, they may have sounded irritated. Therefore, it is not unlikely that Billy may have concluded that Charlie is irritated with them for bringing *another* problem to their door and may themselves have been irritated that Charlie seems dismissive of something that Billy thinks is important. Of course, at this point, neither Billy nor Charlie have actually discussed anything, but are merely reacting to what they perceive about the other person.

From the moment Charlie said 'what is the problem now?' things appeared to unravel very quickly.

Activity

Consider how things may have turned out differently; how would you have handled things if you were Billy or Charlie?

As stated in the previous chapter, it can be quite difficult to step back from the moment, particularly if our emotions are heightened. An alternative course of action might have been for Billy to arrange a pre-booked meeting to discuss their pay rise, as opposed to springing the discussion on a stressed Charlie. Similarly, Charlie might not have jumped to an erroneous conclusion about what Billy wanted to talk about, then persisted with it, despite mounting evidence that Billy was getting irritated and was saying that there was not a 'problem'. Perhaps if Charlie and Billy had a better understanding of each other, or a different relationship, things may have turned out differently. However, even if Billy and Charlie were total strangers, there may have been a different outcome if they both had had an understanding of the themes we will address in this chapter.

Conversations are not all about what we say

It is probably a reasonable assumption that most readers will be familiar with the term 'non-verbal communication'. If you have read the first part of this book, you certainly will be! However, if you skipped that part (of course, we know that you would never do such a thing), here is a very brief recap.

When we think about non-verbal communication, we probably think of those things that might fall under the umbrella of 'body language' and see this as supplementary or as a reinforcer of the words we employ. This is a basic error that we all make; we may choose our words carefully and think that these are what is being *heard*, and in being heard I mean received and understood (Hargie, 2021). Consequently, we can be both surprised and aggrieved when we have skilfully crafted a sentence only for it to seem to have the opposite of its desired effect. However, we may be less surprised about the negligible impact of words if we consider the amount of attention our listener affords the following: actual words – 7%; the way words are delivered (tone, accents on certain words, etc.) – 38%; facial expressions – 55% (Moss, 2017).

Activity

Consider what Charlie's response represents. What part of the delivery might they be reacting to most strongly?

In the case study, Charlie did not appear to be listening to Billy's words, but instead reacted to tone of voice, and possibly facial expressions, all of which were filtered through Charlie's expectation of what Billy was there to talk about and about to say.

As we discussed in the previous chapter, we like to think that we are conscious and alert, and that we process and respond to the information taken in by our senses on the merits of that information. However, we do not: Kahneman (2011) discussed *heuristics*, or the mental shortcuts that the brain takes to process information quickly and provide the basis for action. We discussed the fact that the brain looks for patterns in the information it is receiving, compares it to what it already knows, and proceeds on the basis that the conclusions it has quickly reached are probably going to be accurate most of the time. This can be frustrating if we or the person we are talking to has drawn the wrong conclusions and we end up misunderstanding or being misunderstood. However, the brain allows for this potential inaccuracy as a necessary trade-off for us staying ahead of the game and not having to expend a lot of time and energy working out what to say or do next in any social interaction (MacIntyre et al., 2020).

You have possibly heard that human beings form impressions of a stranger within seconds, and that once formed these impressions can be difficult to shift (Todorov et al., 2009). It is a further example of the brain taking in information, subconsciously comparing it to what it already knows, and acting on that basis. The information that informs these unconscious judgements is not just what we have consciously learnt or decided is correct; it is frequently informed by biases that we do not know we have. Again, Kahneman (2011) is a useful source of wisdom in this regard. The brain has a tendency towards biases which impact upon how we perceive and are perceived. A summary of some of these is as follows:

- *Anchoring bias.* We judge new situations in terms of what we already know
- *Confirmation bias.* We subconsciously filter information to greater weight to evidence that supports our existing belief, or chosen course of action, and give less weight to contradictory information
- *The recency effect.* Information that is fresh in our minds, perhaps from the last person we spoke to, has more impact than information received earlier
- *Repetition bias.* If we see the same messages about an issue or group repeated time and again (perhaps via the media), it can impact how we appraise that issue, group, or individual

Unconscious bias is an example of the manner in which views of which we may be unaware influence our decision-making (Atewologun et al., 2018). This can lead to inadvertent discriminatory or oppressive behaviour, which can be more 'insidious and pervasive than overt racism' (McGregor-Smith, 2017: 2). Hopefully, it is evident why we need to be aware of these covert influences on our interactions with others. But what about when people do have access to the information they need, and one would hope are capable of making rational decisions, but still do things that appear bizarre, illogical, or downright bloody-minded?

Why are people stupid?

You could be forgiven for drawing the conclusion that human beings work on autopilot, are hostage to their emotions, or both. You might also conclude that we are doomed to misunderstand and be misunderstood. Unfortunately, there is a little more bad news to discuss before we can reassure ourselves that all is not lost. Have you ever considered the following, or similar, questions:

- Why don't people change their minds when they have the facts that show they are wrong?
- Why do people say stupid things about stuff they obviously know nothing about?

The answer to both these questions is that 'this is how we are made' or at least how we evolved to manage the complexities of being *hypersociable* animals that live in groups (Mercier & Sperber 2017). Mercier and Sperber conclude that what can seem bewildering and annoying from an intellectual perspective makes perfect sense from a *social interactionist* point of view. Our reluctance to change our minds evolved from the need to stick up for ourselves in social groups where, if we did not, someone else might take advantage of us in the competition for scarce food or other resources. In that context, being assertive and prioritising the winning of an argument over being factually right makes perfect sense. This is why we are very adept in picking holes in what other people say, but do not extend that same skill to ourselves (Kolbert, 2017).

Concerning the second question, 'Why do people say stupid things about stuff they obviously know nothing about?', research tells us that humans tend to think they know about things more than they do (Fernbach & Sloman, 2017; Bailey, 2021; Kahneman et al., 2021). This is why someone may have strong opinions about the England football team manager's tactics despite their only qualifications being the ability to swear at the television during *Match of the Day*. Similarly, we may have strong opinions about everything from immigration to economic policy without having a clue what we are talking about (McIntyre, 2015; Bailey, 2021). This is partly down to confirmation bias, but again the answer largely lies in our high level of interconnectedness as social beings (Kolbert, 2017). In *The Knowledge Illusion: Why We Never Think Alone,* Fernbach and Sloman (2017) argue that, because we have evolved to be highly interactive and collaborative beings, we assume a level of shared knowledge and understanding, which in turn allows us to think we know more about subjects than we actually do. For example, as a man of a certain age, I think I have an understanding of how cars work. Therefore, I may have an opinion as to why my partner's car is currently stationary on the driveway. Rashly, and despite protestations and threats, I may decide to 'have a go' with a set of my dad's spanners and with his 1968 version of the *AA Book of the Car* propped up on the bonnet. You may draw your own conclusions about the likely outcome. However, the point of this example is to illustrate that, although I know a bit about cars, I do not know as much as I think I do. Fernbach and Sloman (2017) refer to this as the 'illusion of explanatory depth'. My partner refers to it as something else.

What this means for our difficult conversations is that people with entrenched views are unlikely to change them when confronted by logical, factual argument. In fact, Gorman and Gorman (2016) demonstrate that, when confronted with facts, people will often become more fixed in their point of view, particularly if they have a strong emotional attachment to it. This illustrates the importance of building relationships with people with whom we disagree. Backing them into a corner and proving that they are 'wrong' is not likely to get us anywhere. This will be addressed later in the chapter, but before we move on to the next section there are some positive suggestions to address the issues we have covered.

Although we get a rush of dopamine when receiving information that appears to confirm our beliefs (Gorman and Gorman, 2016), Fernbach and Sloman (2017) demonstrate that people can be persuaded to consider other perspectives when you ask them to work through the practical implications of their views. For example, what would happen if capital punishment were reintroduced or there was a halt to immigration? When individuals work things out for themselves as opposed to being told or confronted, they become far less vehement and entrenched in their thinking.

As we have discussed, we are far more able to pick holes in someone else's point of view than we are our own. Therefore, the work of Taylor (2013: 65) provides a useful checklist to safeguard against our own biases:

- What benchmarks (anchors) am I using in judging this situation?
- Am I being influenced by my previous experiences?
- Am I being unduly influenced by recent or dramatic events?
- What would it take to change my mind?
- How can I moderate against inappropriate bias?
- How do I know I am giving due consideration to the various sources of information?

Activity

Think back over a conversation that did not go well. Consider whether it would have gone better if you had used Taylor's checklist during the conversation. Would the outcome have been different?

People like to feel hard done-by

Having ended the last section on a positive note, it is time that we return to another dissection of human foibles and irrationalities. In the previous section we discussed the evolutionary origins of our potential to be stubborn and infuriating. Hopefully, in future, if people accuse you of being either, you will be able to blame evolution. But what of our tendency to like a good moan and to want to feel hard done-by? Berne (1968) argued that moaning fulfilled a social function, by giving a shared identity and a sense of common cause between two people. In his book *Games People Play,* Berne illustrated that two people could indulge in a set of interactions that were in many ways predictable and led to a shared feeling, or 'payoff' of feeling aggrieved. He termed this 'game' *'ain't it awful'.* Underlying this and other similar patterns of behaviour was a degree of predictability in human communication that he described in his theoretical framework Transactional Analysis.

Although arguably less popular now than it was in the 1960s through to the 1980s, Transactional Analysis (TA) was very influential as a means of understanding human behaviour through analysing patterns of communication. The predictability in these patterns of communication and behaviour was, according to Berne, the result of us replicating in adult life the feelings and behaviours we learnt as a child. Similarly, sometimes we behave, think, and feel in ways that were copied from parents or other authority figures. Berne called these, respectively, the child and adult *ego states.* If you have ever felt 'naughty', 'small', or 'rebellious' when being spoken to by your boss, this would be an example of the Child ego state. If you have ever caught yourself sounding just like your mother, Berne would argue that this corresponds to the Parent ego state.

What links Berne's TA to what we have previously discussed is his emphasis on communication existing at a psychological level, beneath the surface of the actual words being said. Similarly, in his belief that many conversations followed predictable patterns based on the templates of our learnt behaviour (from childhood or copied from parental figures), Berne showed how conversations can possess an apparent life and momentum of their own, far removed from our conscious intent.

To moderate the influence of Child and Parent ego states, Berne argued that we need to consciously apply our Adult ego state, which he defined as operating in the here and now, rationally processing the information and acting upon it. We might see some parallels with Kahneman's System 2 thinking in Berne's conceptualisation of the Adult ego state. However, Berne's ego states were not rooted in neuroscience; rather, his thinking emerged from a psychoanalytical tradition. However, psychologists have since explored Berne's contention that individuals employ manipulative and destructive 'games' in their interpersonal relationships, that these are the product of learnt behaviour, and that people may not be aware that they are doing so (Hargaden & Sills, 2014; Lac & Donaldson, 2022).

Berne's Transactional Analysis theories developed along several different trajectories. One that is of particular relevance is the Drama Triangle (Karpman, 1968). Karpman used metaphors, drawn from archetypes in fairy tales, to illustrate roles that people can occupy in their interactions with others: Victim (the damsel in distress – note that the roles Karpman identified were not gender-specific); Persecutor (the villain); Rescuer (the hero/heroine). The motives, behaviours, and feelings associated with each role can be summarised as follows:

Victim: Feels hard done-by or acts as if they are helpless. They invite others to feel sorry for them and come to their rescue. However, the reward or payoff for being in the victim role is that of feeling aggrieved and not having to take responsibility, or even make the effort, to make things better. It is for others to change, or to make things different, and until that is achieved the victim cannot be happy. However, the reward in feeling aggrieved is such that the Victim can resent those who try to make things better for them, may sabotage their efforts, move the goal posts, and then blame those who come to their rescue for not helping them. They can then adopt the Persecutor role.

Rescuer: Appears concerned for the Victim, yet their key motive is to feel better about themselves. They may subconsciously both like the feeling of superiority and resent the Victim's 'helplessness'. Consequently, the Rescuer takes over and does not allow the Victim agency in solving their own problem. As the Victim makes greater or shifting demands in their subconscious desire to remain in the Victim role, the Rescuer can be drawn into doing more than they anticipated or are capable of. The Rescuer can then end up frustrated and resentful and adopt either the Victim or Persecutor roles.

Persecutor: In this role the Persecutor also likes to feel aggrieved. Their reward is in identifying faults in others and blaming and punishing them. Like those in the Victim role, the Persecutor feels justified in not changing their own behaviour because the fault always lies with someone else (Lac & Donaldson, 2022).

Activity

Can you think of a conversation when you have taken on either the Victim, Rescuer, or Persecutor role? Why do you think this was the case? What could you have done to change the conversation and step out of the role you have taken on?

You may be able to identify people you know who typically adopt the Victim, Persecutor, or Rescuer roles. However, Karpman believed that individuals can transition between the roles, rapidly in the course of a single conversation. The following case study illustrates the Drama Triangle in action. Here, Billy and Charlie have met after their initial flare up.

Case study: Billy and Charlie – the sequel

Billy: I just wanted to say that I felt very upset. I had been having a really hard day and really didn't need not to feel respected. (Victim)

Charlie: Well, Billy, I am sorry if you feel that way. You know that I respect you. What can we do to make things better? (Rescuer) You know I was having a really bad day, too; it isn't easy you know, and no one ever gives you credit for keeping everything afloat. (Victim)

Billy: Yes, but that doesn't give you the right to take it out on everyone else. (Persecutor)

Charlie: Hang on, that's not fair, I don't do that, you've no idea what I've got to put up with that you don't see. (Victim)

Billy: You seem really upset, Charlie. Everyone wants to help, but you need to let us help you. You can't do this by yourself. (Rescuer)

Charlie: I am *not* really upset. I am quite capable of doing my job, thank you. It doesn't help when you make it harder by moaning about nothing. (Persecutor)

You can probably see how the conversation could proceed from here, with its own energy and momentum, leading to a full-blown argument. Karpman (1968) used the term 'Drama' to indicate the high emotive expression, but also repression, as individuals become stuck or cycle through the various roles. They are trying to get their needs met but, in not being explicit about what these are and by unintentionally employing destructive behaviours to achieve what they want, they are doomed to failure (Lac & Donaldson, 2022).

An alternative to the Drama Triangle is the Winner's Triangle (Burgess, 2005). Here Rescuer, Victim, and Persecutor are replaced, respectively, by Caring, Vulnerable, and Assertive, summarised as follows:

Caring: Although concerned for the vulnerable person, they do not need to rescue a victim to feel good about themselves. They put boundaries around what they are prepared and able to do. They do not take over, unless asked to, but are careful not to dominate and are mindful of not saying or doing anything that might make the other person feel inadequate or helpless. In short, they do *with* rather than do *to.*

Assertive: The person asks for what they want and says no to what they don't want. However, they are alert to not being aggressive or dogmatic and may be flexible. In the 1980s the 'stuck record' method of assertion was very much in fashion. In difficult or heated conversations, this approach consisted of repeating the same phrase or sentence repeatedly until you were 'heard'. This was not assertion; it was passive aggression. Being flexible in the Winner's Triangle recognises others' vulnerabilities and that 'winning' is not achieved by someone else 'losing'.

Vulnerable: The individual acknowledges that they are vulnerable, has feelings, and can be hurt. They know that this is not a weakness that must be disguised by being a Persecutor. Similarly, they acknowledge that there is little to be gained by blaming other people as reason for their own inaction. Consequently, it is fine to seek help and even to recognise that someone else may need to be invited to take over for a while, when we are overwhelmed.

It is worth emphasising that neither the descriptions of the Victim nor Vulnerable roles imply that we should pull ourselves together and learn to fend for ourselves. It is legitimate to feel angry when we have been impacted by injustice or have been hurt by others. Here is a replay of the meeting between Charlie and Billy, but this time through the prism of the Winner's Triangle.

Case study: Billy and Charlie – the sequel ... reimagined

Billy: I just wanted to say that I am sad that we fell out the other day. I didn't really appreciate quite what a horrible day it was, and I suppose our argument didn't help. (Caring)

Charlie: It's OK, how were you to know? To be honest it was all a bit frantic, and I let it get to me, so I am sorry that I wasn't really listening and got the wrong end of the stick. I didn't mean to take it out on you. (Vulnerable)

Billy: You didn't really; I just wanted to ask you something. I was a bit nervous, and it came out the wrong way. (Vulnerable)

Charlie: So, do you think we can have that conversation now? If you'd rather have it later that's fine, but I promise not to be so tetchy. (Caring)

Billy: Well, I wanted to talk to you about a pay rise. I've been on the same grade for a while now and I was wondering if the role could be re-evaluated? (Assertive)

Charlie: OK, well it isn't really my decision, but I am glad that you have asked me. I don't want you to get the wrong end of the stick. I know how hard you work and how important you are to the team, but I will have to sit down with you and work through the job role and person specification to show what is different now to when you first started. They are going to need that in detail and I can't promise anything. (Assertive)

Billy: That's fine, I understand that; let's book a time to do that. I'd be grateful if we can do that soon, although I know you are busy. Would there be time this week? (Assertive)

Charlie: Sure, how about Thursday afternoon? Oh, and Billy, you were right about one thing – I know that I'm not good at letting people help and that must be frustrating (Vulnerable); but I also know that you do more than your fair share and it is not always recognised, so let's sit down on Thursday. (Caring)

So, what else can we do?

At this point we will re-visit and develop some of the themes outlined in the earlier chapter 'How to take the "difficult" out of difficult conversations'.

In their research of businesses in the USA, Patterson et al. (2002) stated that people who were good at forming professional relationships with others were particularly adept at having difficult conversations. Some of this ability seemed natural or innate rather than achieved because of specific training. The conclusions that were reached seem to correlate with what we know about *emotional intelligence*, which includes the ability to: identify and understand feelings in others and ourselves; understand how emotions may be affecting our own and others' behaviour; anticipate our own and others' emotional responses to situations and act accordingly; and being able to manage our own emotions and assist others in managing theirs (Salovey & Mayer, 1990; Goleman, 1998; Morrison, 2007).

Patterson et al. (2002) suggest that in difficult conversations, people interpret what is going on and create a rationale for it. This involves making assumptions about the other person's meaning and motivation. Patterson et al. (2002) called this a 'story', and it is this story that drives how we subsequently feel and act. Patterson et al. (2002) highlight three common stories that align with the Drama Triangle roles of Victim and Persecutor: The Victim Story – 'This Is Not My Fault'; The Villain Story – 'This Is Your Fault'; and The Helpless Story – 'I Can't Do Anything'.

In the previous chapter we discussed how our stress responses tend to make us leap to conclusions, catastrophise, and become defensive. Consequently, to avoid conversations deteriorating, our first task is to 'check our stories': What are we thinking? Is it accurate? How do we know? What alternative story might there be? What do we think the other person's story is? A good place to start is by checking for the Victim, Villain, and Helpless stories.

Recognising the other person's story as well as our own is an example of emotional intelligence in action. A further example is being able to recognise when the other person is becoming stressed or agitated and respond accordingly. When conversations start to deteriorate, we often tend to press on regardless, seemingly oblivious to what is happening around us (Bourne, 2013; Van Heugten, 2018; Forrester et al., 2020). Patterson et al. (2002) argue that for people to have difficult conversations both parties need to feel 'safe'. This does not necessarily mean physical safety, as we discussed in the previous chapter that our stress responses react to verbal or written cues as if they could be a physical threat. Consequently, in difficult conversations, when we are feeling unsafe a typical reaction is 'silence or violence' (Patterson et al., 2002, Major et al., 2013). These are shorthand terms for withdrawing, shutting down, avoidance (silence), and aggression, controlling, and labelling behaviours (violence).

For people to feel safe they need to know that you care about their concerns, and you care about them. If you return to the most recent case study you can see this in action from both Charlie and Billy. A way of establishing or re-establishing safety is to use contrasting statements – a Don't Statement and a Do Statement. Here is an example of an attempt to re-establish safety in the face of defensiveness:

'Look I know this is quite difficult, for both of us, but this is what I am thinking.'

'What I am really not trying to do is to blame you or try and make you or anyone else feel bad for what has happened.' (Don't Statement)

'I just need to make sure that the same thing doesn't happen again in future. We don't have that option. So, I need to know what we can do, but I am not sure what that is. I need your help, so perhaps we can work it through together.' (Do Statement)

These statements also combine the elements of the Winner's Triangle: Caring, Vulnerable, Assertive. Perhaps take a minute to identify them. Variations on the Do and Don't Statements are ones you can do for yourself in preparation for a difficult conversation. If we accept that difficult conversations are likely to be stressful, and knowing what we do about our brain's behaviour under stress, we may then consider the possibility that we possibly lose sight of what we want or need from that conversation. We may get upset or angry, and we may prioritise the short-term gain of winning the argument over getting the result we need. Therefore, before entering a potentially difficult meeting, create your own Don't and Do Statements:

- What do I really need to get out of this meeting?
- What do I really not want to happen?

We have discussed these concepts in our work with a variety of individuals and groups. The feedback has been that, even when highly stressed, individuals have been able to use their Do and Don't Statements as a kind of anchor to keep them focused. Returning to the first and second case studies, consider how things may have turned out differently if Billy had prepared some Do and Don't Statements. Similarly, would things have deteriorated if

Billy and Charlie had been able and willing to recognise issues of safety and respond accordingly?

Conclusion

In the next chapter we will bring together some of the themes we have discussed in this and the previous chapter. We will use as our backdrop a typical 'bad day' at work. We will also introduce some new concepts that will build upon and consolidate what we have covered so far. Before we do, here is a summary of some of the key points from this chapter.

Key takeaways

- Human beings are not always likely to change their minds about something when they are presented with new information
- In difficult conversations, people may become more intransigent when logic and rational arguments are used
- Under stress, people lose sight of their longer-term goals and become focused on winning the argument
- Compile Do and Don't Statements to stay focused
- The Drama Triangle (Karpman, 1968) is a useful means of analysing destructive behaviours in difficult conversations. The Winner's Triangle (Burgess, 2005) is a useful alternative

References

Atewologun, D., Cornish, T., & Tresh, F. (2018). *Unconscious bias training: An assessment of the evidence for effectiveness*. Equality and Human Rights Commission Research Report 113.

Bailey, J.J. (2021). False beliefs and the illusion of explanatory depth. *Journal of Business and Behavioral Sciences, 33*(2), 54–64.

Berne, E. (1968). *Games people play: The psychology of human relationships* (Vol. 2768). Harmondsworth: Penguin.

Bourne, I. (2013). *Facing danger in the helping professions: A skilled approach*. Maidenhead: Open University Press.

Burgess, R.C. (2005). A model for enhancing individual and organisational learning of emotional intelligence: The Drama and Winner's Triangles. *Social Work Education, 24*(1), 97–112.

Fernbach, P., & Sloman, S. (2017). *The knowledge illusion: Why we never think alone.* New York: Penguin.

Forrester, D., Killian, M., Westlake, D., & Sheehan, L. (2020). Patterns of practice: An exploratory factor analysis of child and family social worker skills. *Child & Family Social Work, 25*(1), 108–117.

Goleman, D. (1998). *Working with emotional intelligence.* London: Bloomsbury.

Gorman, S.E., & Gorman, J.M. (2016). *Denying to the grave: Why we ignore the facts that will save us.* Oxford: Oxford University Press.

Hargaden, H., & Sills, C. (2014). *Transactional analysis: A relational perspective.* London: Routledge.

Hargie, O. (2021). *Skilled interpersonal communication: Research, theory and practice.* London: Routledge.

Karpman, S. (1968). Fairy tales and script drama analysis. *Transactional Analysis Bulletin, 7*(26), 39–43.

Kahneman, D. (2011). *Thinking, fast and slow.* New York: Allen Lane.

Kahneman, D., Lovallo, D., & Sibony, O. (2019). A structured approach to strategic decisions. *MIT Sloan Management Review.*

Kahneman, D., Sibony, O., & Sunstein, C.R. (2021). *Noise: A flaw in human judgment.* London: Hachette.

Kolbert, E. (2017). Why facts don't change our minds. *The New Yorker, 27*, 47.

Lac, A., & Donaldson, C.D. (2022). Development and validation of the Drama Triangle Scale: Are you a victim, rescuer, or persecutor? *Journal of Interpersonal Violence, 37*(7–8).

MacIntyre, P.D., Wang, L., & Khajavy, G.H. (2020). Thinking fast and slow about willingness to communicate: A two-systems view. *Eurasian Journal of Applied Linguistics, 6*(3), 443–458.

Major, K., Abderrahman, E.A., & Sweeney, J.I. (2013). 'Crucial conversations' in the workplace. *AJN: The American Journal of Nursing, 113*(4), 66–70.

Mann, S. (2014). *Emotion: All That Matters.* London: Hodder & Stoughton.

McGregor-Smith, R. (2017). *Race in the workplace: The McGregor-Smith review.* Report for Department for Business, Energy and Industrial Strategy. https://assets. publishing. service. gov. uk/government/uploads/system/uploads/attachment_ data/file/594336/race-inworkplace-mcgregor-smith-review.pdf.

McIntyre, L. (2015). *Respecting truth: Willful ignorance in the Internet age.* New York: Routledge.

Mercier, H., & Sperber, D. (2017). *The enigma of reason.* Cambridge, MA: Harvard University Press.

Morrison, T. (2007). Emotional intelligence, emotion and social work: Context, characteristics, complications and contribution. *British Journal of Social Work, 37*(2), 245–263.

Moss, B. (2017). *Communication skills in health and social care.* London: Sage.

Patterson, K., Grenny, J., McMillan, R., & Switzler, A. (2002). *Crucial conversations: Tools for talking when stakes are high.* New York: McGraw-Hill Education.

Patton, B. (2017). You can't win by avoiding difficult conversations. *Journal of Business & Industrial Marketing, 21*(4).

Ross, J.W. (2016). *Specialist communication skills for social workers: Developing professional capability.* Basingstoke: Palgrave Macmillan.

Salovey, P., & Mayer, J. (1990) Emotional intelligence. *Imagination, Cognition, and Personality, 9*(3), 185–211.

Stone, D., Heen, S., & Patton, B. (2010). *Difficult conversations: How to discuss what matters most.* Penguin.

Taylor, B. (2013). *Professional decision making and risk in social work.* Exeter: Learning Matters.

Todorov, A., Pakrashi, M., & Oosterhof, N.N. (2009). Evaluating faces on trustworthiness after minimal time exposure. *Social Cognition, 27*(6), 813–833.

Van Heugten, K. (2018). Inter-personal and organisational aggression in human services following a community disaster. *The British Journal of Social Work, 48*(6), 1682–1699.

7

'Charlie is having a bad day!' A case study

Introduction

This chapter will return to some of the themes addressed in the previous two chapters. In addition, it will introduce some new concepts, which will consolidate and extend what has already been discussed. We will explore:

- Emotional contagion
- How electronic communication can go wrong and what you can do about it
- How fatigue and our internal body clock can impact upon our discussions
- How fear of losing can impair our ability to negotiate

To illustrate these themes and to give them a context, they have been located in an extended case study of a fictional 'bad day'. It is not autobiographical (not much), but we suspect that the events being described are ones that the reader can relate to. You may have had some or all of these experiences; hopefully not all on the same day!

Early morning

The day begins after a restless night; Charlie has not been sleeping well. They are used to poor sleep and, like many people, are not particularly concerned (Walker, 2017). Work has been particularly stressful, and Charlie has been drinking more alcohol than usual. Their drinking is not excessive, and Charlie has found that a couple of drinks helps them get off to sleep, instead of lying in bed and ruminating on the night just gone and the day ahead. However, the anaesthetic effect of alcohol comes at a cost: drinking less than 2 units of alcohol decreases sleep quality by 9.3%; 2 units by 24%; and more than 2 by 39.2% (Stein & Friedmann, 2006; Pietilä et al., 2018).

DOI: 10.4324/9781003433248-9

The impact on sleep quality will have cognitive impacts later in the day. At the moment, although Charlie is experiencing 'brain fog', they anticipate that a few coffees will give them the necessary boost they need to deal with work. The recommended amount of sleep for an adult is 7–9 hours (Watson et al., 2015). Charlie has only been sleeping about 5–6 hours a night for the past two weeks or so. What they are not aware of is that this sleep loss has a significant effect on cognitive performance; their sleep loss over the past ten days means that their brain is functioning as if it has been awake for 24 hours. This will have an impact on Charlie's ability to think and make decisions as the day unfolds.

In addition to reduced cognitive performance, sleep loss and fatigue will make Charlie more irritable and anxious than they would be normally, and this is not ideal preparation for the difficult conversations that the day has in store. Similarly, Charlie's level of fatigue will mean that they will have difficulty adapting to abnormal or changing situations and will become dogmatic and fixed in their thinking when they will need to navigate some sensitive negotiations later in the afternoon (Walker, 2017).

Activity

Consider a time when you have not had enough sleep. Do you recognise the feelings described above? Make a list of the ways in which lack of sleep impacts on your ability to concentrate and communicate effectively. For example, do you find it hard to focus? Make decisions? Process what is being said to you?

At work: And so it begins

As usual, Charlie begins the working day by diving straight into their emails. They find that answering the seemingly constant flow of emails is almost a full-time job in itself. However, they pride themselves on answering promptly and hope that this enables them to stay on top of everything. However, things never seem to work out that way. By mid-morning, Charlie is experiencing the email flow as something of a torrent; they do not seem to be able to focus on any one thing without someone asking them to sort out something trivial or having to deal with others' apparent stupidity. Charlie is already tired and irritable because of sleep deprivation, which is not helping matters. This makes it difficult to gain a sense of perspective and to prioritise. Like many people, Charlie finds themself rushed and struggling to catch up. Research has identified this as a common theme in workers' relationships with email (Dürscheid et al., 2013). This means that when Charlie has difficult conversations later in the day, they will be feeling rushed and distracted, which means that they may miss the early verbal and non-verbal cues that indicate that things are not going according to plan and that the other person is feeling 'unsafe' (Patterson et al., 2002). In addition, Charlie may unwittingly project their stress and anxiety onto others.

A useful addition to our knowledge about stress is the notion of emotion contagion (Hatfield et al., 1993). As social animals, human beings are configured to pick up and mirror the emotional states of others. This is why laughing is infectious; why some people can 'lift a room', just as others can suck the energy out of it. Leaders (this includes those who others instinctively look to or defer to, not just those who hold leadership positions) are particularly emotionally contagious: a stressed leader can make others feel stressed; conversely, they can be a calming and stabilising influence (Barsade et al., 2018; Clarkson et al., 2020).

When Charlie meets Chloe: Emotion contagion in action

It is 10 in the morning and Charlie is already feeling very stressed. Their colleague, Chloe, is by nature a generally calm person. She is also feeling in a good mood, having won £10 in the office lottery syndicate, and because the person she least likes in the office is off today after being bitten by their neighbour's cat. Chloe is thinking of using the £10 to buy the cat a present. Chloe does have a slight sense of trepidation as she must discuss some tricky budget figures with Charlie, who is not known for their grasp of financial detail.

Charlie is evidently agitated; they are speaking quite quickly and breathlessly. After a minute or so with Charlie, Chloe finds herself feeling quite anxious: her breathing gets shallower, and she begins talking quickly to mirror Charlie. She is finding it difficult to explain the complexities of the budget issue and keeps getting the information in the wrong order. It is evident that Charlie is not understanding what Chloe is saying. Therefore, Chloe leaves feeling exasperated, saying that she will resolve the issue and let Charlie know when she has.

What is going on in this example of emotion contagion?

Although probably slightly exaggerated in terms of the speed and level of escalation, this is an example of the emotion contagion that we have seen replicated in large meetings and in a on-on-one situation. In this example, Charlie and Chloe are, to an extent, reflecting and amplifying each other's emotional states. If you recognise this happening, a useful tip in these situations is to slow down! Deliberately focus on breathing slowly and steadily and concentrate on not speaking at the other person's pace. This is a very simple technique, but it works. If you persist you may find that the other person or people start slowing down, too. This is an invaluable skill for staying calm in difficult conversations.

You may also find that some people will, consciously or unwittingly, speak quickly as a destabilising tactic. They may accompany this with rapid questions. Again, try not to get drawn in; we need to speak at thinking pace, not the other way around.

Charlie and Chloe: Reimagined

Charlie and Chloe meet to discuss finances. Charlie is quite agitated and stressed; they would prefer not to discuss the budget now. However, being aware of their potential impact on others, Charlie focuses on breathing and speaking slowly and finds themselves calming down enough to listen to what Chloe is saying.

Alternatively, Chloe refuses to get caught up in Charlie's stress and speaks calmly and slowly so that at least Charlie has been told what they need to hear.

Activity

If you are aware that you are about to embark on a stressful or difficult conversation, take two deep breaths before beginning the conversation. Breathe in for a count of 7 and out for a count of 11. Focus on the counting – not the content of the conversation. This can distract your brain from believing you are 'under threat' and prevent a flight, fight, freeze reaction.

Gaining control of the start of the day

Earlier chapters have referred to locus of control and discussed the importance of control in relation to stress. Research by Karasek (1979) and then Theorell (2020) concluded that it was not necessarily high workload that accounted for most workplace stress; it was a combination of high demand, low support, and feeling as though you are not in control. Charlie's way of dealing with emails and other demands being fired at them is almost guaranteed to make them stressed. Charlie has a strong belief in their ability to multitask. However, the ability to multitask is largely misunderstood and surrounded in myth. In reality, doing several things at once means that we do them less well than if we focus on one thing. This contributes to cognitive overload, stress, and poor performance (Rosen, 2008; Srna et al., 2018; Crenshaw, 2021). We know that Charlie begins the day by diving straight into their emails. By doing so they set up the conditions for being quickly overwhelmed. This is probably a common experience for many of us, but it does not need to be this way.

For once, Charlie starts the day with a clear head

On arrival at work, and before opening their emails, Charlie spends a few minutes reviewing what they need to get done before the end of the day. They spend some time making and ordering their 'to do' list and reviewing what they were not able to get done the previous day. Instead of being constantly available on email, they limit this to certain times of the day and book this into their online calendar. They have immobilised the pop-ups and notifications on their computer, as they have found that being constantly reminded that they have mail is distracting and causes them stress (Knapp & Zeratsky, 2018). This is an alternative way of working; it is not perfect, and it is not a fail-safe way of avoiding becoming overwhelmed. However, it does give you a fighting chance. Unfortunately, Charlie has yet to learn this.

Mid-morning: Drowning in emails

Who doesn't love an email?

Perhaps, like us, you view email as something of a mixed blessing: on the one hand it enables us to communicate instantaneously with individuals or groups; on the other, emails increase our ability to be misunderstood. A body of research has tracked the evolution of CMC or 'computer-mediated communication' (Dürscheid et al., 2013). This has focused on the way emails and other forms of CMC (texts and social media) have affected the way we communicate, the language that is used, but also, critically, how we perceive others through the prism of electronic communication media. Baeva (2016) argues that email transforms an individual from a 'real person' to a virtual one. This can depersonalise and result in a deterioration of empathic connection (Ogwu et al., 2020). In addition, emails and other forms of electronic communications deprive us of the interpersonal cues derived from observation of the other person, their tone of voice, gesture, and body language (Morgan et al., 2014). Critically, this impacts on our ability to pick up the early warning signals of irritation and anxiety that are crucial in enabling us to avoid potential conflict. In fact, Morgan et al. (2014) conclude that this impacts upon trust, what Patterson et al. (2002) would refer to as 'safety'.

Our view about emails is that, in the absence of more reliable information, we substitute our own interpretations, what Patterson et al. (2002) would call 'stories', of the other person's meaning, plus their intentions and feelings towards us. We often say that we do not read emails, we *hear* them. For example, emails can be brief and to the point. It is easy to substitute a tone of voice and conclude that the sender is irritated, officious, or condescending. This is our *interpretation* and, for the reasons we have discussed in other chapters, this is a very rapid and often subconscious appraisal; it may not be accurate.

In addition, the pace at which emails confront us with new information, the way we must rapidly refocus our attention as we quickly move from one topic to another, causes cognitive strain, fatigue, and contributes to a sense of being out of control (Brown et al., 2014). This is compounded by the fact that studies have shown that it takes us longer to process information from a screen than paper (Clinton, 2019). Consider this in the context of our understanding of Kahneman's System 1 thinking and the way our defensive stress responses are triggered by the brain's ability to leap to conclusions based on partial information. We can see that the conditions are there to be misunderstood and for communications to unwittingly provoke.

Charlie has an email spat

Charlie has received a two-line email from a colleague. They want to know when Charlie will have a report ready and ask if Charlie could confirm a date.

Charlie had previously said that the report would be ready by the end of the week, but it will be late because of the pressure of work. The email has irritated Charlie because it has prompted them to feel both stressed and a little inadequate because they are behind schedule. Of course, Charlie's colleague knows nothing of this. Because they too are struggling with the pressure of work, they had missed or forgotten the email where Charlie had confirmed a deadline for the report. Because they too are stressed and busy, they had sent a quick email to Charlie without any greetings or other non-factual content.

Charlie does not know that their colleague is similarly stressed and, crucially, does not take a moment to consider this and how it might have influenced the email. Instead, Charlie has interpreted a tone of voice in their colleague's email that was both critical and officious. Charlie quickly replied: 'As I already told you, the report will be ready by Friday. Sending me officious emails is not going to make it happen any sooner.'

Activity

At this point, consider how you would respond to Charlie.

The colleague could have phoned Charlie. They could have sent an email suggesting that they had been misunderstood and perhaps they could speak in person. They could respond to Charlie's rude tone. It may be worth revisiting the Drama Triangle, discussed in the previous chapter, because the ensuing dialogue followed a pattern where both parties alternated between Victim and Persecutor and became increasingly rude and attacking. You may have experience of similar email dialogue. If so, we are sure that you can imagine the content and trajectory of the email spat between Charlie and their colleague. It does not have to be this way.

Emails: Handle with care

Emails and other forms of electronic communication provide immediate person-to-person contact that is unconstrained by the necessity of physical proximity. That immediacy can make us forget that we do not actually have to respond straight away. It can be more difficult to defuse face-to-face encounters just by slowing things down and delaying our responses. For the reasons highlighted in the previous two chapters, 'slow it down' would be my number one tip for taking the heat out of situations, unless you feel that the situation may escalate and get out of hand without your intervention. This also gives time to engage the brain whilst considering a response. However, what I have learnt is that for particularly stress-inducing emails, it is not helpful to delay considering a response until the next day, or even much later in the same day. This creates the conditions for rumination and for the offending email to unnecessarily create lingering stress and anxiety. It is better to craft a response, but not send immediately. We have often been surprised, when returning to draft responses that we believed were thoughtful and measured, that they are not the exemplars of diplomacy, tact, and calm authority that we thought they were. At this point, we hope that we do not need to say that sending emails late at night is a bad idea; similarly, sending emails when we believe that our vocabulary, sincerity, and fluency have been 'enhanced' by alcohol is a recipe for disaster.

You may have received unpleasant emails where the sender has unnecessarily pressed the 'Reply all' button. There are several potential reasons for them doing this: they feel they need to bring the gang along to provide strength in numbers; they hope that others will leap in and rough you up; or they are showing off. There may be other, less malign, intentions, but let us focus on these.

'Reply all' presents a conundrum: if you respond, copying in everyone, you are showing that you mean business and are not about to be pushed around. However, you are then slipping into a fight–flight scenario where, as we have seen, the brain's focus on a short-term goal of 'winning' can be compounded by not wanting to lose face. These imperatives also apply to the protagonist. As we discussed in the previous chapter, getting into a fight is not going to be helpful in achieving any positive result. One thing that we have found helpful when metaphorically getting ready to roll up our sleeves and get into an argument is to remember that we are at work, and this is a job. This may seem a deceptively simple idea, but it helps maintain emotional distance and a sense of perspective. This is not to deny one's own feelings or to tacitly accept that it is part of the working environment to be an 'emotional trashcan' for others' frustrations and insecurities (Shaffer, 2010; McDermott & Lachlan, 2021). For this approach to work, it is necessary to create and attempt to maintain boundaries and deal with the unpleasant reality that unpleasant emails can be deliberate attempts to unsettle, intimidate, and anger.

To understand these methods in action, it is again worth returning to the 'relationships' chapter, particularly those sections focusing on Victim and Persecutor dynamics. Before responding to an email, it is worthwhile quickly analysing it for Victim–Persecutor clues and/or considering the issue of 'safety' as defined by Patterson et al. (2002). Although he is referring to face-to-face verbal communication, the work of Braithwaite (2002) is helpful in understanding aggressive email exchanges. He argues that the aggressor, perhaps subconsciously, is attempting to snare us on 'verbal hooks', including criticism and insults. Braithwaite suggests that we tend to respond to the words without analysing and addressing the behavioural intent behind them. For example, we may unwittingly slip into defending ourselves against baseless accusatory statements. For the aggressor, this is a wonderful diversionary tactic, and it also lures you into a potential fight. This may be the aggressor's intention all along. A useful tip, which also works in verbal interactions, is to check for *projection*, where the other person accuses you of the feelings they are experiencing, for example, saying that you are angry when it is in fact they who are displaying anger. Although these projections and other behaviours are hurtful, they frequently fulfil a defensive function (Schimel et al., 2003). The issue of 'safety', as discussed in the previous chapter, may be relevant here (Patterson et al., 2002). Nevertheless, Braithwaite (2002) argues that it is nearly impossible to move a situation on without dealing assertively with this behaviour, and suggests the following formula:

1. Make a statement about the behaviour
2. State the impact of the behaviour upon you
3. Request the behaviour to stop
4. Return to the issue or change the subject

(Braithwaite, 2002: 20)

Is this best done with a 'Reply all' email? Absolutely not. You may be concerned about not appearing sufficiently assertive but, return to the helpful aide-mémoire: this is work; it is not a chest-beating contest.

Our advice is always, where possible, not to engage in difficult dialogue by email for the reasons highlighted in this chapter. However, what of the bystanders, the often-unwitting contributors to the unfolding email drama? They may be tempted to try and rescue the situation or add their own grievances into the mix: these are the perfect conditions for a full-blown Drama

Triangle. The social worker Kieran O'Hagan talked about 'flamethrowers' – people who were on the edge of a heated conversation but who, sometimes unwittingly, intervened and made the situation worse. Following O'Hagan's advice, it is best to address these people separately, invite them to talk to you, but not in the free-for-all of a group discussion (O'Hagan, 1986).

As you may have gathered, we spend a lot of time on email, but it is worth devoting some attention to electronic communication because of its ubiquity in professional life. Before we move on to Charlie's afternoon (it does not get any better) we would like to share with you a valuable lesson from history. It is a case study in how to respond to communications when tensions are running high.

Case study: It is 1962 – do we start a war or not?

In 1962, the United States and Soviet Russia came close to nuclear war. This was in an era before email and even before a 'hotline' had been established between Washington and the Kremlin to defuse potential crises. Both the USA and Russia were deeply suspicious of each other's motives and intentions. In a parallel with the issues we have discussed in the previous three chapters, both sides were trying to find clues about each other based on the interpretation of partial information and in the context of high stress: one false move could lead to nuclear war.

Amid escalating tensions, the Russian leader sent a conciliatory letter to the Americans. Whilst the Americans were pondering how to reply, external events deteriorated further. The Russians then sent a second letter that was far more belligerent in tone. The Americans were very alarmed. Their generals pressed for an equally aggressive response; fearing that Russia was about to launch a nuclear strike, some in the American military wanted to bomb the Russians first.

The American President John F. Kennedy and his advisors resisted the pressure to start a war and chose to ignore the most recent, aggressive Russian letter. Instead, they responded to the first conciliatory message with a conciliatory letter of their own. There were many heroes on both sides in 1962; they were the ones who did not let their fears overrule their heads. However, that one act by Kennedy and his advisors may well have saved the world from nuclear destruction.

If we thought Charlie was having a bad day, at least it was not *this* bad. Fortunately, few days at the office lead to nuclear holocaust (although some days this seems like a distinct possibility). You may therefore wonder what the relevance is of events long ago to our more mundane working lives. The lesson we take from this, and it is one that has stood us in good stead, is that if events are running away with you, if you have come late to an email trail where things are getting progressively more heated and belligerent, then – if you can – take a step back and respond to the less emotionally charged or provocative communication that may be further back in the email chain. Try it – it does not always work but you will be surprised how often it does.

The afternoon: Things do not get any better

We have previously discussed the impact of tiredness on cognitive performance, and we know that Charlie is tired, grumpy, and is having the sort of day where, when they leave work at the end of it, they are unlikely to be punching the air with the sheer joy of being alive. Before that moment comes, Charlie has a big meeting scheduled for 4pm. Charlie does not know this, but in terms of cognitive functioning and attention span, this is perhaps the worst time in the day to schedule an important event. There are two things that are not working in Charlie's favour and, for that matter, any of the other participants: *decision fatigue* and *our alertness*.

Decision fatigue

It is estimated that an adult in societies like the United States and Europe makes 35,000 decisions a day (Sollisch, 2016). These decisions can be simple ones: Do I wear a tie to work? Does it make me look serious or stuffy? Does it make me look like the chap in the psychopath drama on the TV? Alternatively, do I have breakfast or, instead, stuff myself with chocolate bars on the train to work? That is a relatively simple decision – chocolate wins every time.

There are obviously more important decisions that we need to make, but they all require energy and effort. Unfortunately, our ability to make decisions deteriorates as the day goes on: our capacity to regulate our behaviour and not just take the easy option gets worse; this is what is called *decision fatigue* (Pignatiello et al., 2020). What this means is that, as we make more and more decisions, we are more likely to feel irritated and physically tired. Crucially we are also more likely to avoid making difficult decisions, to go along with things that we might otherwise disagree with, be impulsive, and, in general, make worse decisions. In something of a perfect storm, the peak conditions for decision fatigue collide with the impact of our circadian rhythms, or body clocks.

Circadian rhythm and alertness

After a slow start most people's mental alertness peaks in late morning (there are of course 'early birds' and 'night owls' who follow a different pattern). Our alertness then dips markedly in the afternoon for a second, though less significant, peak in the early to mid-evening (Walker, 2017). In short, 4pm is not the ideal time to be having a meeting.

Activity

Check your work calendar for the next month and, wherever possible, move important meetings to the morning (or the time you know you are most alert).

The big meeting: Disaster in the afternoon

Charlie is chairing a meeting to negotiate a contract with an external service. Charlie has not been having the best of days and they are not in the mood to be messed around. They are feeling tired but have had a lot of coffee and are feeling confident. The representative of the service provider is known for being quite awkward and likes to show off how clever they are. Today Charlie does not have the patience: they are anticipating a struggle and decide to be tough. The contractor presents their case and comes up with some suggested costs. Although not quite grasping the detail, Charlie thinks it best to ask some difficult questions; they are combative and are pleased that they are scoring points in the negotiation, which is making the contractor revise their offer.

The meeting drags on. Charlie is enjoying feeling in charge, but after an hour they are conscious that there is no conclusion; other people in the meeting are looking disinterested and bored; and even Charlie's interest is waning.

The contractor comes back with yet another set of calculations. Wearily both Charlie and their colleagues agree to these. Charlie did not fully understand what was going on, but was pleased that they held their own and after the meeting said so to a colleague, who replied: 'The trouble is, Charlie, I think we just agreed to what they first proposed an hour ago: I think this is a worse deal than we had at the beginning, but I don't think we actually have any of this written down.'

Negotiating styles

Shell (2006) identifies five negotiation styles and suggests that individuals may have a strong preference for a particular approach or approaches. Some individuals enjoy the competition of negotiation; they literally 'play to win'. In employing a competing style, negotiators may well secure an initial perception of victory. However, this may be to the detriment of the relationship with the other party. This appears to be the strategy employed by Charlie.

A competitive approach may be favoured by individuals who wish to establish and maintain control. Yet, the impression of control and confidence can be illusory. Insecurity and anxiety may be revealed by a lack of willingness to depart from a narrowly defined agenda. Similarly, there may be a refusal to acknowledge perspectives, other than one's own. Gabriel (1998) suggests that the fear of losing control is a key determinant of managers' actions. In the case study, Charlie appeared to be judging the success of the negotiation in terms of how they felt about themselves rather than the outcome.

Perhaps diametrically opposed to the competing style is the avoiding style. Avoiders are not confident and dislike negotiation; they are more likely to skirt around potentially contentious or conflictual issues. Shell (2006) identifies Accommodators as individuals who value relationships and enjoy problem-solving. The inherent risk of this approach is that the individual can be too accommodating and may feel taken advantage of. This feeling may be particularly acute following an encounter with another individual who adopts a more competitive style. Similarly, Compromisers may too readily give concessions that may be regretted later. However, where there is fundamental disagreement between parties, willingness to compromise, at least to a certain degree, is probably essential to avoid deadlock.

105

Finally, the Collaborators' approach appears to be attractive if a high value is placed upon empathising with the perspectives of others and working out complex issues together. However, there is a risk that negotiation can get bogged down in the complexity of detail, if an attempt is made to reach a consensus on a myriad of issues, where there may be fundamental disagreement. Occasionally, parties may have to 'agree to disagree' and accept that not all issues can be resolved by consensus.

Shell (2006) argues that successful negotiators ask more questions than poor negotiators. The purpose of these questions is to understand the other party's views, values, and anxieties. A successful negotiator aims for an empathic understanding of the other individual's perspective. Of course, this does not just involve asking questions; active listening and other displays of empathy are crucial to a successful negotiation.

Once an agreement has been reached, mechanisms should be in place to ensure that the parties involved in a negotiation fully understand precisely what has been agreed, and that the record of the agreement and any actions arising from it are unambiguous. However, it is possible for both parties to come away from a negotiation with subtly, and occasionally radically, different interpretations of what was said and agreed. Pressure of time, and possibly the relief at reaching agreement, may result in insufficient attention being paid to accurate phrasing and recording the nature of the agreement. This is what happened in the example.

Activity

Work out what your negotiating style is and *practise*.

Home again: A conclusion (of sorts)

After working late again, Charlie finally returns home to their loving family who are engrossed in watching *Bake a Celebrity*. Consequently, Charlie is largely ignored, apart from being told by them that Charlie had forgotten to put the bins out this morning. This triggers an argument in which even the dog is involved, barking at anyone and everyone. Charlie remembers that they once read something about a 'Drama Triangle', but that is another story.

Key takeaways

- Sleep loss and fatigue have an impact on cognitive abilities
- Emotion contagion makes us vulnerable to mirroring the stressed emotional states of others. We may be similarly contagious
- Be aware of the emotional impact of emails
- Create a strategy to manage emails
- Consider your default negotiating style

References

Baeva, L.V. (2016). Virtual communication: Strengthening of real relationships or simulation? *International Journal of Technoethics (IJT)*, *7*(1), 51–61.

Barsade, S.G., Coutifaris, C.G., & Pillemer, J. (2018). Emotional contagion in organizational life. *Research in Organizational Behavior*, *38*, 137–151.

Braithwaite, R. (2002). *Managing aggression*. London: Routledge.

Brown, R., Duck, J., & Jimmieson, N. (2014). E-mail in the workplace: The role of stress appraisals and normative response pressure in the relationship between e-mail stressors and employee strain. *International Journal of Stress Management*, *21*(4), 325.

Clarkson, B.G., Wagstaff, C.R., Arthur, C.A., & Thelwell, R.C. (2020). Leadership and the contagion of affective phenomena: A systematic review and mini meta-analysis. *European Journal of Social Psychology*, *50*(1), 61–80.

Clinton, V. (2019). Reading from paper compared to screens: A systematic review and meta-analysis. *Journal of Research in Reading*, *42*(2), 288–325.

Crenshaw, D. (2021). *The myth of multitasking: How 'doing it all' gets nothing done*. Coral Gables, FL: Mango Media.

Dürscheid, C., Frehner, C., Herring, S.C., Stein, D., & Virtanen, T. (2013). Email communication. *Handbooks of Pragmatics [HOPS]*, *9*, 35–54.

Gabriel, Y. (1998). Psychoanalytic contributions to the study of the emotional life of corporations. *Administration and Society*, *30*(3), 291–314.

Hatfield, E., Cacioppo, J.T., & Rapson, R.L. (1993). *Emotional contagion*. Cambridge: Cambridge University Press.

Karasek Jr, R.A. (1979). Job demands, job decision latitude, and mental strain: Implications for job redesign. *Administrative Science Quarterly*, 285–308.

Knapp, J., & Zeratsky, J. (2018). *Make time: How to focus on what matters every day*. New York: Crown Currency.

McDermott, K.C., & Lachlan, K.A. (2021). Emotional manipulation and task distraction as strategy: The effects of insulting trash talk on motivation and performance in a competitive setting. *Communication Studies*, *72*(5), 915–936.

Morgan, L., Paucar-Caceres, A., & Wright, G. (2014). Leading effective global virtual teams: The consequences of methods of communication. *Systemic Practice and Action Research, 27,* 607–624.

Ogwu, S., Sice, P., Keogh, S., & Goodlet, C. (2020). An exploratory study of the application of mindsight in email communication. *Heliyon, 6*(7).

O'Hagan, K. (1986). *Crisis intervention in social services.* London: Palgrave Macmillan.

Patterson, K., Grenny, J., McMillan, R., & Switzler, A. (2002). *Crucial conversations: Tools for talking when stakes are high.* New York: McGraw-Hill Education.

Pietilä, J., Helander, E., Korhonen, I., Myllymäki, T., Kujala, U.M., & Lindholm, H. (2018). Acute effect of alcohol intake on cardiovascular autonomic regulation during the first hours of sleep in a large real-world sample of Finnish employees: Observational study. *JMIR Mental Health, 5*(1), e23.

Pignatiello, G.A., Martin, R.J., & Hickman Jr, R.L. (2020). Decision fatigue: A conceptual analysis. *Journal of Health Psychology, 25*(1), 123–135.

Rosen, C. (2008). The myth of multitasking. *The New Atlantis, 20,* 105–110.

Schimel, J., Greenberg, J., & Martens, A. (2003). Evidence that projection of a feared trait can serve a defensive function. *Personality and Social Psychology Bulletin, 29*(8), 969–979.

Shaffer, G. (2010). *Taking out your emotional trash: Face Your feelings and build healthy relationships.* New York: Harvest House Publishers.

Shell, R. (2006). *Bargaining for advantage: Negotiating strategies for reasonable people.* New York: Penguin Books.

Sollisch, J. (2016). The cure for decision fatigue. *Wall Street Journal,* 10.

Srna, S., Schrift, R.Y., & Zauberman, G. (2018). The illusion of multitasking and its positive effect on performance. *Psychological Science, 29*(12), 1942–1955.

Stein, M.D., & Friedmann, P.D. (2006). Disturbed sleep and its relationship to alcohol use. *Substance Abuse, 26*(1), 1–13.

Theorell, T. (2020). The demand control support work stress model. In T. Theorell (Ed.), *Handbook of socioeconomic determinants of occupational health: From macro-level to micro-level evidence* (pp. 339–353). Cham: Springer.

Walker, M. (2017). *Why we sleep: Unlocking the power of sleep and dreams.* London: Simon & Schuster.

Watson N.F., et al. (2015). Recommended amount of sleep for a healthy adult: A joint consensus statement of the American Academy of Sleep Medicine and Sleep Research Society. *Sleep, 38*(6), 843–844.

Part 3

How to talk about what really matters

8

Communication in context

Introduction

This chapter will explore the challenges professionals face in having difficult conversations; how organisational cultures and societal expectation provide a difficult and occasionally impossible burden of expectation on individuals who, no matter how skilled, committed, and diligent, possess the same human fallibilities as the rest of the population. The specific focus is on health and social care practice, but the key themes are transferrable to a range of other occupations.

🔍 Case study: (Not) speaking out

Just after midnight, on 5 May 2007, Kenya Airlines Flight 507 took off from Douala Airport in Cameroon bound for Nairobi, Kenya. Within minutes, the plane had crashed a few miles south of the airport. There were no survivors. Cited as one of the contributory factors in the crash was the apparent unwillingness of the co-pilot to challenge the captain when it became evident that the plane was in danger. A similar situation was replicated in two fatal crashes in Tokyo and San Francisco, respectively: subordinate crew members did nothing when the captain's actions were clearly going to lead to an accident.

What links all three crashes is that the investigators highlighted dominating power relationships, an unwillingness of highly skilled professionals to challenge those further up the hierarchy, and an underpinning assumption that the 'boss knows best'. It is perhaps unsurprising that a study of flight deck communication found that subordinates frequently use 'hints' rather than more direct communication to point out their captain's errors (Fischer & Orasanu, 1999). In addition, numerous air crash investigations have highlighted an over-reliance and over-confidence in procedures and technology

DOI: 10.4324/9781003433248-11

to keep planes and passengers safe (Taylor et al., 2020). Even in a field as technically and as procedurally dependent as aviation, there is no substitute for people talking to each other and, occasionally, being prepared to challenge.

You may wonder what relevance air crashes have to the fields of health, social care, and education. Successive investigations into catastrophic errors and systemic failures in health and social care have highlighted similar issues to those highlighted by air crash investigators. In Britain, the Francis Report (2010) into the Mid-Staffordshire NHS Trust scandal highlighted a hierarchical culture sustained by bullying, where staff were afraid to speak out. Seven years previously, Lord Laming's investigation into the death of seven-year-old Victoria Climbié revealed that the junior social worker, at the heart of the case, referred to her manager as 'the headmistress': 'I was a child who was seen but not heard, and had seen what had happened to those who challenged [the manager]' (Laming, 2003: 192). Yet, the final Laming Report (2003) appeared not to adequately address the psycho-social aspects of the case, specifically the impact of toxic interpersonal relations and dominating power relationships (Ferguson, 2005). Instead, its conclusions largely focused on 'doing the simple things properly' (Laming, 2003: 105). Arguably, the potential effectiveness of the Laming and other similar inquiries has been limited by their assumptions: that complex, emotionally challenging and occasionally frightening work can be made safer and error-free with a greater focus on doing the basics and by refining and implementing policies and processes.

Many investigations appear to be largely detached from an understanding of the impact of human psychological factors on safe practice (Ferguson, 2005; Dustin, 2016; Masson & Parton, 2020). A key theme of many investigations into accidents, tragedies, and scandals has been a focus on what has gone wrong, not why (Ferguson, 2005; Reason, 2016); a frequent conclusion being that professionals need to be better at sharing information, following procedures, and, in the case of child protection, communicating with service-users in a sufficiently authoritative manner (Masson & Parton, 2020; Forrester, 2024). Until relatively recently, what has been absent in inquiry reports and practice responses has been sufficient consideration of why intelligent, conscientious, caring professionals do not speak up and speak out when they know something is wrong. Policy responses have typically emphasised procedural and regulatory solutions to ensure that 'this must never happen again' (Rogowski, 2020). This is an impossible goal; no system is 100% secure, and the real world cannot be made risk- and error-free. Practice is made more unsafe without sufficient acknowl- edgement and accommodation of the human factors that contribute to accidents and individual and systemic failings of practice. Consequently, phrases such as 'insufficient professional curiosity', 'disguised compliance', and the 'rule of optimism' perhaps only serve to reinforce a popular view of professionals as gullible dupes, lacking courage, and failing in their basic duties (Jones, 2014).

The evolution of social work practice with children and families

With an extract from an NSPCC practice manual (1904: 7–8), Ferguson (2011) gives a fascinating insight into the challenging world of child protection work- ers in the early 1900s:

> As to the necessary access to the house where the ill-used child dwells, this too will, like getting access to the child, depend on determination and tact … two can generally play at the game of bounce and the owner of the house plays it with all the odds on his side.

The 'game of bounce' refers to the adversarial experience of trying to gain access to a child in the face of parental resistance: something that will still be familiar to social workers in the twenty-first century (Ferguson, 2011).

Moving forward in time, the end of the Second World War heralded an era of optimism for children's social work (Lynch, 2020). In addition to being academically highly qualified, it was envisaged that the primarily female workforce in the new Children's Departments would bring qualities seen as essentially feminine, the ability to engage with others and 'to set both chil- dren and adults at their ease' (Curtis Report, 1946: para. 446).

Although, they present a highly gendered picture of professional prac- tice, both the NSPCC manual and the later Curtis Report encapsulate the potentially conflicting imperatives in social work practice: the need to exer- cise authority in situations of conflict, yet demonstrate compassion, care, and empathy. These may be familiar to readers as the 'care versus control' dilemma (Ruch, 2012; Green & Carey, 2013; Thompson, 2024). Arguably, in the twenty-first century these tensions have still not been resolved.

As social work practice evolved, the 'home visit' became central to most forms of social work intervention with families (Ferguson, 2011). In parallel, social work training developed by focusing on counselling skills; and more recently, upon anti-oppressive and anti-discriminatory practice. What was missing was adequate recognition of just how difficult it is to work with people who do not want you in their lives and who certainly do not want you in their home (Forrester, 2024). In part, this was founded on an essentially optimistic vision of the place of social work in society. The 1968 Seebohm Report laid the foundations of the modern social services departments. Its underpinning vision was one where people would be grateful to have the help of social workers. This was revisited in the 1982 Barclay Report, with its conceptualisation of social workers as helpful, community-based change agents (Rogowski, 2020). As recently as the late 1990s, when I was a practice teacher, I recall listening with increasing incredulity to a social work educator as he highlighted his vision of social workers and service users uniting in a common cause against 'the system' and assumedly marching arm in arm to the sunlit uplands of utopian socialism.

This naivety and muddled understanding of what social workers do and face was illustrated in the responses to numerous investigations into child deaths throughout the 1980s and 1990s. Social workers were portrayed as incompetent and cowardly in their apparent inability to keep children safe (Ferguson, 2005; Jones, 2014; Rogowski, 2020). Yet, closer reading of case reviews or inquiries revealed professionals struggling in the face of overt and covert intimidation, threats, and actual violence and determined efforts by parents to obstruct social workers in the performance of their duties (Ferguson, 2011; Jones, 2014; Ferguson et al., 2021). In essence, not much appeared to have changed since the publication of the NSPCC handbook in 1904.

Despite the lofty ideals of both the Curtis Report of 1946 and the later Seebohm Report of 1968, throughout the 1970s and into the twenty-first century social work maintained a poor reputation among the public, press, and politicians. Social workers have been portrayed as 'bungling do-gooders' on one hand and, paradoxically, as 'interfering busybodies' on the other (Rogowski, 2020). Arguably this reflects the ongoing tension between the conflicting imperatives of care and control, which impacts on the difficult discussions professionals are required to have. This will be discussed later in this chapter, but let us first turn to the impact on difficult conversations in the professional cultures of nursing and medicine.

The good nurse and the good doctor

Perhaps until recently, many in social work may have envied the esteem in which doctors and nurses were held. However, the mantra of 'doctor knows best' reflected a paternalistic and hierarchical culture that placed patient autonomy in a subordinate position to professional expertise and status (Seaton, 2023). A consequence of this power differential was that many doctors avoided having a difficult conversation with a patient about their diagnosis, particularly if the diagnosis was life-changing or terminal. This approach was not necessarily a product of professional condescension; nor avoidance or lack of courage on the part of the physician. Instead, it typically originated from the desire to spare the patient potential harm or distress (Tabak et al., 2012). In most, although not all, countries it is now generally accepted that patients are entitled to the truth about their diagnoses, but there are still many reasons why doctors may be reluctant to be completely honest about what they reveal. Firstly, by not revealing information, physicians may maintain the impression of being the expert 'good doctor' worthy of the patient's and their family's trust (Sarafis et al., 2014; Genuis, 2021). Similarly, many physicians may be reluctant to take hope away from the patient, believing that it may accelerate psychological and physical decline (Tabak et al., 2012). Other medical professionals may struggle with the individual, emotional impact of giving patients distressing news, perhaps erroneously believing that specific guidelines or procedures will offer some buffer (Sarafis et al., 2014; Brouwer et al., 2021).

The findings of research conducted with doctors resonate with the concept of emotional labour, which involves managing one's own and others' emotions to correspond with the expected requirements of the job (Hochschild, 2012). Hochschild suggested that many occupations that embody 'masculine' values of stoicism and emotional restraint required practitioners to behave in an emotionally neutral or overtly detached manner in the face of distressing situations. In contrast, occupations that typically employed women were often associated with nurturing and caring expressions of emotion. Nevertheless, although nursing is frequently perceived and accepted as a 'feminised' profession, emotional detachment is integral to the contemporary notion of the 'professional' nurse (Meerabeau & Page, 1998). However, nurses forced to become emotionally neutral, when they preferred to be emotionally supportive, experienced 'outlaw emotions' of shame, guilt, and inadequacy

(Burfoot, 1994); in short, being required to emotionally detach from patients had negative effects for nurses (Aitken et al., 2002; Ziarat et al., 2023).

Leigh (2013) provides a different perspective; exploring the concept of 'emotional distancing' as a protective strategy for health care professionals. Although the concept remains ill defined, several studies have identified reduced emotional exhaustion and increased ability to display empathy towards patients, amongst nurses who are able to maintain emotional detachment (Kim, et al., 2020). Interestingly, what is missing from the literature review conducted by Kim et al., is an understanding of how emotional distancing is received by patients and their families.

In essence, emotional distancing aligns with research into professional resilience. For example, Badger et al. (2008: 70) suggests that resilient professionals are: 'walking an internal tightrope between empathetic connection with patients and families and emotional separation'. Similarly, in their research into social worker resilience, Grant and Kinman (2018) concluded that resilient individuals can be upset, stressed, distressed, moved, but they do not get overwhelmed.

The understanding of resilience as outlined by Grant and Kinman is arguably a little more multifaceted and complex than mere 'emotional distancing', and once we engage with that complexity it is necessary to also understand the impact of concepts such as burnout, psychological defence mechanisms, and the impact of working with risk in conditions of anxiety, stress, and work overload. Unfortunately, these are outside of the scope of this chapter. However, these factors do affect professionals' communication and, in particular, difficult conversations, even determining whether those conversations take place at all.

Of course, the experiences of employees do not exist in isolation and cannot be divorced from the organisational and professional cultures in which they take place. On first reading it may appear that the circumstances of social care and health professionals may differ, health professionals being afforded more deference and public respect, with social care workers occupying a more ambiguous and contested position. This would be misleading. Firstly, the authority of medical professionals is no longer unquestioned but, critically, both health and social care professionals typically work in situations of risk and uncertainty, where both individual and organisational errors can have severe consequences. Critically, communication failures can undermine organisational effectiveness but also lead to catastrophic consequences.

Organisational dysfunction: The role of communication

In the early 1960s Isabel Menzies Lyth published a groundbreaking study of the ward culture and behaviour and attitudes of nurses. Menzies Lyth (1960) noted that leaders (senior nurses) perpetuated the existing rigid, hierarchical work culture by holding essentially negative views of their subordinates, which led to a consistent underestimation of their juniors' capabilities and limited the possibility for change in the organisation. Similarly, junior and student nurses managed their anxieties about being responsible for patients by emotionally distancing themselves from them, deflecting decision-making upwards into the organisational hierarchy, and being overly dependent on procedures as a means of feeling psychologically safe. The anxieties and internal conflicts that nurses felt were frequently deflected through blaming others.

What was absent in the rigid hierarchical system of the hospital was a means of dealing with conflict and anxiety in a productive way. Within a business environment, Lencioni (2012) noted that many organisations harbour an implicit fear of potential conflict: appropriate and healthy challenge is seen as destabilising and something to be supressed. Consequently, members of dysfunctional teams are reluctant to address difficult issues and to appropriately challenge themselves or others. Instead, within these organisational cultures, interpersonal dramas (Karpman, 1968) represent a manifestation of supressed conflict (Regier, 2017). As such, they are a means of conflict *performance* where more overt forms of conflict recognition and resolution are underdeveloped (Huber, 2023). Similarly, Schaef and Fassel (1988) noted a tendency for employees to complain to each other, rather than report or attempt to address problems in the workplace, and to cover up quite significant issues for fear of blame or generating further conflict. Consequently, leaders were often unaware of systemic problems that could lead to organisational dysfunction or even catastrophic failure.

Organisational cultures where difficult conversations are discouraged or actively suppressed create the latent conditions for individual or institutional failure. The term 'groupthink' coined by Janis (1972, 2008) suggested that, in many teams or groups of people, the desire to maintain group cohesion, to 'not rock the boat', can give an illusion of group consensus because people are reluctant to ask difficult questions or have the challenging conversations. This is particularly apparent in highly stressful work environments where groups are making high stakes decisions in conditions of uncertainty and pressure. More alarming is 'wilful blindness' where individuals know what they are doing or seeing is wrong, but either do nothing or rationalise their own inaction as being for the best, often the 'greater good' (Heffernan, 2011).

If they lead to catastrophic consequences these phenomena may appear shocking. For example, it has been argued that groupthink led to staff at NASA not having the challenging discussions that might have prevented the Challenger Space Shuttle disaster (Esser & Lindoerfer, 1989; Dimitroff et al., 2005). Nevertheless, many of the apparent lapses of professionalism, the failure to act and the failure to ask difficult questions, cannot easily be dismissed as deficiencies of the individual; often they are very human responses to working in complex, stressful, and demanding situations. In social care, the Laming Report may have concluded that the death of Victoria Climbié could have been prevented by 'doing the simple things properly' (Laming, 2003: 105); yet at the time of Victoria's death, her social worker had logged ten weeks' worth of unpaid overtime (Laming, 2003). This was someone who was working very hard. As stated in the introduction, successive inquiries into failings in health and social care practice have failed to adequately address the reasons why individuals are fallible and the impact of working with complexity and risk, in high-pressure working environments.

Working with risk, uncertainty, and anxiety

Risk assessment and management has become a defining feature of health and social care practice (Kemshall, 2016). Yet this exists within a context where there is an unreasonable societal expectation that risk can be eliminated, and that if it is not, then this is the result of human error or negligence (Reason, 2016). Over 30 years ago, Mary Douglas provided a succinct description of what we might characterise as 'blame culture': 'The (system) we are in now is almost ready to treat every death as chargeable to someone's account, every accident as caused by someone's criminal negligence, every sickness a threatened prosecution. Whose fault? is the first question' (Douglas, 1992: 15–16).

Reason (2016) argues that it is convenient for organisations and society to identify and blame individuals for errors, accidents, and tragedies because it avoids the necessity of addressing the more complex underlying issues that led to these incidents. Furthermore, Reason's research reveals that those individuals who are often blamed following a serious incident are frequently the unwitting inheritors of what he terms 'an accident sequence' – a domino effect of events over which the person may have little influence and of which they may be unaware. The consequence of this for many professionals is that they work within an organisational or societal culture where they are vulnerable to being blamed for things that they may not control (Leigh & Leigh, 2017; Parker & Davies, 2020). Feeling a loss of control is a key source of stress (Theorell, 2020). Loss of control is in turn exacerbated by overwork and mental overload (Bunting, 2011; Wirz et al., 2018; Goldsby et al., 2020; Briker et al., 2021). This is a toxic combination of factors which negatively impacts the quality of communication between professionals and between professionals and service-users/ patients. Anxious and stressed practitioners often find themselves trying to have challenging conversations with anxious and stressed patients or service-users (Petitta et al., 2017; Barsade et al., 2018).

The aftermath of many inquiries into organisational failings emphasises the need for 'better communication' (Ferguson, 2011; Burgener, 2020; Rogowski, 2020). However, these inquiries often do not consider the difficulties, and the skills required to have challenging discussions (Forrester, 2024), instead largely focusing on the need to share information between professionals. However, as Ferguson (2011) points out, sharing information is all very well, but it requires someone to process and conceptualise that information for it to have any beneficial impact.

Following the death of Victoria Climbié, the UK Government's Every Child Matters initiative established protocols for information sharing (Department of Health, 2003). Many organisations invested heavily in digital methods of information sharing and storage. However, Miller (2024) cautions against over-reliance on digital systems as a panacea for communication issues; there is a difference between communication and understanding, and understanding and effective intervention. Unless these differences are understood and addressed, one can be left merely with a digital record of actions leading up to, but not preventing, an accident (Dekker, 2014). Consequently, information sharing can give a false sense of security. Cynically, it can reinforce a sense that blame can be shared if things go wrong.

As previously discussed, Menzies Lyth's study of nurses in the 1960s revealed a reluctance to take responsibility and a delegation of decision-making responsibility up the hierarchy. In addition, Menzies Lyth reported an over-reliance on procedures as a defence mechanism against anxiety. For different reasons, the airliner accidents referred to in the introduction to this chapter revealed a similar pattern of unhealthy hierarchical deference and over-reliance on procedures. Procedural responses to practice challenges may be essential in promoting efficiency and equity. However, they may also be limiting: they can reinforce what Langer (1989) terms as *mindlessness*. In essence, familiarity and repetition of experiences can lead to a narrow focus on 'getting the job done', which in turn links to routinised responses to novel situations.

Communication in context: Difficult conversations

Forrester (2024) researched children and families' social workers' communication styles when having difficult conversations with parents. It was notable that both the parents and the social workers appeared to be having parallel discussions. The social workers largely focused on giving instructions, in short, telling people what they needed to do. Parents' anxieties and concerns were often missed or received cursory attention; there was little evidence of empathy or a collaborative approach to problem-solving. In earlier research, Gallagher et al. (2012) discovered that, following discussions with social workers, service-users reported struggling to understand what was happening to them and why, and there was evidence that service users and professionals often had divergent understanding of what had been agreed and what actions would be taken.

Ferguson (2011) argues that the language that is used to frame social work intervention, the focus on 'need' and 'partnership', is often at odds with the realities of practice. In particular, it has obscured the difficulties of working with hostile and resistant families. Forrester (2024) suggests that, following the death of Peter Connelly, there was an increased focus on 'authoritative' and more directive forms of social work intervention. In addition, overworked, stressed practitioners working within a blame culture are more likely to adopt risk-averse and routinised approaches to practice (Masson & Parton, 2020; Brearley, 2023).

Forrester (2024) makes the point that social work practitioners are rarely trained to have the challenging conversations that are central to their everyday experience of practice. This appears to be the case with healthcare practitioners. Nevertheless, Pettit and Stephen (2015) view the ability to have challenging conversations as integral to the delivery of compassionate care.

This, in part, is informed by the lessons from the Francis Report (2010) into the failings of Mid-Staffordshire NHS Trust. However, Pettit and Stephen also see that having the capability to have challenging conversations is a necessary component of nurse resilience. Similarly, research with medical students highlighted their unpreparedness for the challenging conversations they face and their desire to have training incorporated into the curriculum.

Conclusion

The central premise of this chapter is that it is impossible to employ the skills required to have challenging and difficult discussions without understanding the organisational and societal context in which they take place. This book largely focuses on understanding ourselves and others, in particular the hidden drivers of our behaviour and attitudes. However, we hope that this chapter has given you an insight into how organisational and professional cultures may influence the conduct of individuals in ways that they may not be aware of. In addition, our aim was to illustrate why, after an accident or high-profile event of organisational and professional failure, merely calling for better communication between professionals or between agencies will achieve little. A focus on what went wrong without a deep understanding of why is guaranteed to ensure that 'lessons will *not* be learned'.

Key takeaways

- Communication between both individuals and agencies is heavily influenced by organisational and professional cultures. The impact of these may be underestimated by those working in the professions or organisations
- Working in situations of high risk, uncertainty, and with anxiety around the attribution of blame will have an impact on how professionals communicate
- The impact of these factors is often insufficiently recognised or understood when investigating accidents and individual or organisational failure. Consequently, without this understanding, the risks of these events happening again is exacerbated.

References

Aitken, L.H., Clarke, S.P., Sloane, D.M., Solchalski, J., & Silber, J.H. (2002). Hospital nurse staffing and patient mortality, nurse burnout and job dissatisfaction. *Journal of the American Medical Association, 288*(16), 1987–1993.

Badger, K., Royse, D., & Craig, C. (2008). Hospital social workers and indirect trauma exposure: An exploratory study of contributing factors. *Health & Social Work, 33*(1), 63–71.

Barsade, S.G., Coutifaris, C.G., & Pillemer, J. (2018). Emotional contagion in organizational life. *Research in Organizational Behavior, 38*, 137–151.

Brearley, C.P. (2023). *Risk and social work*. London: Routledge.

Briker, R., Walter, F., & Cole, M.S. (2021). Hurry up! The role of supervisors' time urgency and self-perceived status for autocratic leadership and subordinates' well-being. *Personnel Psychology, 74*(1), 55–76.

Brouwer, M.A., Maeckelberghe, E.L., van der Heide, A., Hein, I.M., & Verhagen, E.A. (2021). Breaking bad news: What parents would like you to know. *Archives of Disease in Childhood, 106*(3), 276–281.

Bunting, M. (2011). *Willing Slaves: How the Overwork Culture Is Ruling Our Lives*. London: HarperCollins UK.

Burfoot, J.H. (1994). *Outlaw emotions and the sensual dynamics of compassion: The case of emotion as instigator of social change*. Burlington, VT: Middleton College.

Burgener, A.M. (2020). Enhancing communication to improve patient safety and to increase patient satisfaction. *The Health Care Manager, 39*(3), 128–132.

Curtis Report. (1946). *Care of Children: Interdepartment Committee Report*. Curtis Committee Cmd6922, London HMSO.

Dekker, S.W. (2014). The bureaucratization of safety. *Safety Science, 70*, 348–357.

Department of Health. (2003). *Every Child Matters*. Stationery Office, London.

Dimitroff, R.D., Schmidt, L.A., & Bond, T.D. (2005). Organizational behavior and disaster: A study of conflict at NASA. *Project Management Journal, 36*(2), 28–38.

Douglas, M. (1992). Risk as a forensic resource. *Daedalus, 119*(4), 1–16.

Dustin, D. (2016). *The McDonaldization of social work*. London: Routledge.

Esser, J.K., & Lindoerfer, J.S. (1989). Groupthink and the space shuttle Challenger accident: Toward a quantitative case analysis. *Journal of Behavioral Decision Making, 2*(3), 167–177.

Ferguson, H. (2005). Working with violence, the emotions and the psycho-social dynamics of child protection: Reflections on the Victoria Climbié case. *Social Work Education, 24*(7), 781–795.

Ferguson, H. (2011). *Child protection practice*. London: Bloomsbury.

Ferguson, H., Disney, T., Warwick, L., Leigh, J., Cooner, T.S., & Beddoe, L. (2021). Hostile relationships in social work practice: Anxiety, hate and conflict in long-term work with involuntary service users. *Journal of Social Work Practice, 35*(1), 19–37.

Fischer, U., & Orasanu, J. (1999). Confronting the boss indirectly: Study of cockpit crews finds copilots use 'hints' to correct captains. *Research News & Publications Office*. Georgia Institute of Technology.

Forrester, D. (2024). *The enlightened social worker: An introduction to rights-focused practice.* Bristol: Policy Press.

Gallagher, M., Wosu, H., Stewart, J., Cree, V.E., Hunter, S., Evans, S., Montgomery, C., Holiday, S., & Wilkinson, H. (2012). Engaging with involuntary service users in social work: Findings from a knowledge exchange project. *British Journal of Social Work, 42*(8), 1460–1477.

Genuis, Q.I. (2021). A genealogy of autonomy: Freedom, paternalism, and the future of the doctor–patient relationship. *The Journal of Medicine and Philosophy: A Forum for Bioethics and Philosophy of Medicine, 46*(3), 330–349.

Goldsby, E., Goldsby, M., Neck, C.B., & Neck, C.P. (2020). Under pressure: Time management, self-leadership, and the nurse manager. *Administrative Sciences, 10*(3), 38.

Grant, L., & Kinman, G. (Eds.). (2018). *Developing resilience for social work practice.* London: Bloomsbury.

Green, L., & Carey, M. (Eds.). (2013). *Practical social work ethics: Complex dilemmas within applied social care.* Farnham: Ashgate.

Heffernan, M. (2011). *Wilful blindness: Why we ignore the obvious.* New York: Simon & Schuster.

Hochschild, A.R. (2012). *The managed heart: Commercialization of human feeling.* Berkeley, CA: University of California Press.

Huber, M. (2023). *Resilience in the team: Ideas and application concepts for team development.* London: Springer Nature.

Janis, I.L. (1972). *Victims of groupthink.* Boston, MA: Houghton Mifflin.

Janis, I.L. (2008). Groupthink. *IEEE Engineering Management Review, 36*(1), 36.

Jones, R. (2014). *The story of Baby P: Setting the record straight.* Bristol: Policy Press.

Karpman, S. (1968). Fairy tales and script drama analysis. *Transactional Analysis Bulletin, 7*(26), 39–43.

Kemshall, H. (2016). Risk, social policy, welfare and social work. In A. Burgess, A. Alemanno, & J. Zinn (Eds.), *Routledge handbook of risk studies* (pp. 252–261). London: Routledge.

Kim, J., Kim, S., & Byun, M. (2020, November). Emotional distancing in nursing: A concept analysis. *Nursing Forum, 55*(4), 595–602.

Laming, H. (2003) The Victoria Climbié Inquiry, Stationery Office, London.

Langer, E.J. (1989). Minding matters: The consequences of mindlessness–mindfulness. In *Advances in experimental social psychology* (Vol. 22, pp. 137–173). San Diego, CA: Academic Press.

Leigh, H. (2013). *The patient: Biological, psychological, and social dimensions of medical practice.* New York: Springer Science & Business Media.

Leigh, J., & Leigh, J. (2017). *Blame, culture and child protection.* Basingstoke: Palgrave Macmillan.

Lencioni, P.M. (2012). *The five dysfunctions of a team: Team assessment.* San Francisco, CA: Wiley & Sons.

Lynch, G. (2020). Pathways to the 1946 Curtis Report and the post-war reconstruction of children's out-of-home care. *Contemporary British History, 34*(1), 22–43.

Masson, J., & Parton, N. (2020). England: Attempting to learn from mistakes in an increasingly 'risk averse' professional context. In K. Biesel, J. Masson, N. Parton, & T. Pösö (Eds.), *Errors and mistakes in child protection* (pp. 35–54). Bristol: Policy Press.

Meerabeau, L., & Page, S. (1998). 'Getting the job done': Emotion management and cardiopulmonary resuscitation in nursing. In G. Bendelow & S.J Williams (Eds.), *Emotions in social life: Critical themes and contemporary* issues. London: Routledge.

Menzies Lyth, I. (1960). Social systems as a defence against anxiety: An empirical study of the nursing service of a general hospital. *Human Relations, 13*(2), 95–121.

Menzies Lyth, I. (1988). *Containing anxiety in institutions: Selected essays, Vol. 1.* London: Free Association Books.

Miller, C. (2024). The myth of the digital panacea. *Writing for Digital Media.*

Muzicant, & Peled, E. (2018). Home visits in social work: From disembodiment to embodied presence. *British Journal of Social Work, 48*(3), 826–842.

Parker, J., & Davies, B. (2020). No blame no gain? From a no blame culture to a responsibility culture in medicine. *Journal of Applied Philosophy, 37*(4), 646–660.

Pettit, A., & Stephen, R. (2015). *Supporting health visitors and fostering resilience: Literature review.* London: Institute of Health Visiting.

Petitta, L., Jiang, L., & Härtel, C.E. (2017). Emotional contagion and burnout among nurses and doctors: Do joy and anger from different sources of stakeholders matter? *Stress and Health, 33*(4), 358–369.

Reason, J. (2016). *Organizational accidents revisited.* London: CRC Press.

Regier, N. (2017). *Conflict without casualties: A field guide for leading with compassionate accountability.* New York: Berrett-Koehler Publishers.

Rogowski, S. (2020). *Social work: The rise and fall of a profession?* Bristol: Policy Press.

Ruch, G. (2012). Where have all the feelings gone? Developing reflective and relationship-based management in child-care social work. *British Journal of Social Work, 42*(7), 1315–1332.

Sarafis, P., Tsounis, A., Malliarou, M., & Lahana, E. (2014). Disclosing the truth: A dilemma between instilling hope and respecting patient autonomy in everyday clinical practice. *Global Journal of Health Science, 6*(2), 128.

Schaef, A.W., & Fassel, D. (1988). *The addictive organization.* New York: Harper & Row.

Seaton, A. (2023). *Our NHS: A history of Britain's best loved institution.* New Haven, CT: Yale University Press.

Tabak, N., Itzhaki, M., Sharon, D., & Barnoy, S. (2012). Intentions of nurses and nursing students to tell the whole truth to patients and family members. *Journal of Clinical Nursing, 22*(9–10), 1434–1441.

Taylor, C., Keller, J., Fanjoy, R.O., & Mendonca, F.C. (2020). An exploratory study of automation errors in Part 91 Operations. *Journal of Aviation/Aerospace Education & Research, 29*(1), 33–48.

Theorell, T. (2020). Job demand/control/strain. In M.D. Gellman (Ed.), *Encyclopedia of behavioral medicine* (pp. 1254–1257). Cham: Springer.

Thompson, N. (2024). *Understanding social work: Preparing for practice*. London: Bloomsbury.

Warner, J. (2015). *The emotional politics of social work and child protection*. Bristol: Policy Press.

Wirz, L., Bogdanov, M., & Schwabe, L. (2018). Habits under stress: Mechanistic insights across different types of learning. *Current Opinion in Behavioral Sciences, 20*, 9–16.

Ziarat, H.M., Seyedfatemi, N., Mardani-Hamooleh, M., Farahani, M.A., & Vedadhir, A. (2023). Nursing in oncology ward with intertwined roles: A focused ethnography. *BMC Nursing, 22*(1), 83.

9

How to talk about sexuality and gender

Rylee Spooner

Introduction

Sexuality and gender are ever-evolving worlds and becoming more present in our societal consciousness. For those who don't identify as LGBTQ+, this world can be daunting and feel difficult to talk about for fear of saying the wrong thing. But also, we must consider that conversations about sexuality and gender can be tricky even when they do not relate to queer issues (famously, the birds and the bees!). This chapter aims to educate you on current language, coming out, taboos, and how to sensitively navigate conversations on this topic.

A whistlestop tour of language

This chapter will not *only* focus on LGBTQ+ topics, but it is important to address the language I will be using throughout. Before we can even begin to talk about communication around LGBTQ+ experiences, the language around this topic needs to be clarified. It can feel overwhelming, especially if you are less well versed in LGBTQ+ culture. Hopefully, however, the below list will give you some clarity of language used for queer identity and societal queer discourse. Having said that, this chapter is not an educational guide on gender and sexuality, so please research further on terminology and identities with which you are less familiar.

Let's start with *the* acronym – LGBTQ+. Or, as my grandad calls it, the alphabet people.

L is for lesbian

A woman who is emotionally, romantically, or sexually attracted to other women. Lesbians can also identify as non-binary; therefore the attraction isn't 'exclusive' to women.

DOI: 10.4324/9781003433248-12

G is for gay

A term primarily used to describe men who are emotionally, romantically, or sexually attracted to other men. However, gay is often used as an umbrella term to include lesbians and bisexuals.

B is for bisexual

Someone who is emotionally, romantically, or sexually attracted to two or more genders.

T is for transgender

Transgender (sometimes styled as trans*) is when someone's assigned sex at birth does not match their gender identity. Trans* people can transition, internally, socially, medically/physically, and/or legally.

Q is for queer

Queer is a term that has been reclaimed by some, not all, LGBTQ+ individuals as an umbrella term for diverse sexualities and gender identities. As a term, 'queer' encompasses various identities outside of heterosexuality and cisgender. Queer is also a political identity – to be queer you must advocate for the liberation of all oppressed groups.

And the '+' is for...

Asexual

A person who experiences little to no sexual attraction to others. Yet, they may experience romantic or emotional attractions. Asexuality is a broad spectrum (check out Yasmin Benoit's activist work for more on asexuality!)

Non-binary

A gender identity that does not exclusively fit within the categories of male or female. Non-binary individuals may identify as a combination of genders, as neither exclusively male or female, or as entirely separate from the concept of gender.

Intersex

People born with physical sex characteristics (such as chromosomes, genitals, or reproductive anatomy) that do not fit typical binary notions of male or female.

Questioning

This refers to individuals who are exploring their sexual orientation or gender identity and are not yet sure where they fit within the LGBTQ+ spectrum.

Other terms that will be used throughout this chapter are...

Cisgender

When someone's gender identity matches their assigned sex at birth.

Ally(ship)

Being an ally is *actively* advocating for and supporting minoritised or marginalised groups that you do not belong to – more on that later.

Cisgenderism

A cultural and systemic ideology that stigmatises and denies gender identities outside of the norm of men and women. This belief values cisgender people and expression over trans* identities and expression, or even those who dress in a gender non-conforming way.

Heteronormativity

Much like cisgenderism, heteronormativity is the presumption that all people are heterosexual, thus perpetuating that heterosexuality is normal and all other sexual orientations are 'abnormal'. Heteronormativity is not only cultural but also systemic.

Internalised homophobia/transphobia

When one has internalised society's negative views towards transgender or gay people, one may feel negatively about their queer identity. This can lead to feelings of shame and self-hate.

Homophobia/biphobia/transphobia (HBT)

Dislike, prejudice, and/or active discrimination against LGBTQ+ individuals. This can be from a microaggression level to more overt discrimination (e.g., refusal to rent to gay couples)

Deadnaming

This term describes referring to a trans* individual by the name they no longer go by. Intentional deadnaming is a recognised form of transphobia.

Gender affirmation

For trans* individuals, this is the ability to feel affirmed as their gender identity. This is personal to each and everyone. For some, it could be changing their name legally or shaving their hair differently.

Misgendering

Misgendering is when you refer to someone as the wrong gender. This could be through using words such as lady or gentleman, he instead of she, they instead of he, girl instead of boy, etc.

So, why is language so important?

Dear reader, sadly I do not know you! But I can make an assumption here: you *probably* like to be referred to by your name, or nickname. I can also presume that you might not like being referred to as 'mister' if you are a 'miss' (and vice versa). What I am trying to say is, the importance of language, and respecting language, does not only benefit those who identify themselves as queer. When someone gets married and changes their surname, most of their friends and family adjust quickly and refer to them by their new name. Yet, many struggle to respect the same wishes of trans* individuals who change their name or have changed their pronouns.

Current legislation

At the time of writing, there is an ongoing controversy over the Cass Review, Florida's 'Don't say gay' bill, and the new trans* guidance for educators

129

in the UK. One section of the new guidance proposes that if a student requests to socially transition, they should be cautious and make the student wait to make sure this is the right choice. Furthermore, parents should be consulted by the schools before the decision is made. Whilst parents should be kept in the loop about their students at school, this essentially means that students will be outed to their parents. This could pose a threat to those students who have transphobic families. A recent study conducted by The Index on Censorship (2024) found that 53% of librarians polled had been asked to remove books that included LGBTQ+ content. In more than half of those cases, the librarians complied, and those books have been taken off shelves. This is an unfortunate mirror image of Section 28 (revoked over 20 years ago!).

For trans* individuals, especially youth, the future is uncertain, and currently looking bleak. Much of the rhetoric seen in the media is rehashing homophobic sentiment that was prevalent during the 1980s in the face of the AIDS pandemic. In the last five years in England and Wales, the Home Office (2023) has reported a 186% increase in hate crimes against trans people and a 112% increase in hate crimes based on sexual orientation. This is just to give you further context on why navigating topics on gender and sexuality should be met with sensitivity.

Challenging hegemonic views

There is an unfortunate intersection of misogyny, homophobia, biphobia, and transphobia, meaning that there is a dogmatic idea of what is 'normal'. Now, in the global North, this 'normal' is traditionally cisgender, heterosexual, and monogamous, with women taking on more traditional roles of housework and men being seen as the breadwinner. Whilst, undeniably, this narrative has changed, it is still seen as the default. Therefore, when gay couples have access to marriage, and trans* people are subverting established gender norms, people begin to worry about the status quo. This is especially true for biological essentialists who prioritise biological makeup over the lived experiences and emotions of individuals.

Let's put two of these myths around gender to rest! This may help you tackle possible biases you hold or give you the confidence to tackle any remarks you hear as a form of active allyship.

'But there are only two genders!'

Gender is separate to sex. Even so, there is now understanding that the binary sexes of male and female are not so simply categorised. We get taught at school about XY and XX chromosomes, but many biologists have denied that sex is that simple (Fausto-Sterling, 1993). Neuroscientists have now proposed that our brains are more like 'mosaics' of female-typical and male-typical features (Joel, 2021). By only using binary models of sex and gender, it contributes to the pathologisation of trans* and intersex individuals (Cameron & Stinson, 2019). Around 1.7% of infants are born with intersex traits, according to United Nations Free & Equal (n.d.). This estimate nearly matches the amount of red-haired people in the general population! To become more acquainted with this area, I strongly recommend reading up on Anne Fausto-Sterling's work. She is a biologist who has heavily published on the complexity of biology, sex, and gender.

'Trans is new!'

Trans* people are not new. Research demonstrates that over 150 pre-colonial Native American tribes acknowledged third genders within their communities. However, many of the acknowledged gender-variant identities were eradicated through the colonisation of these communities. It is well documented that Indigenous communities have a 'third gender' known as two-spirited people. Colonialism enforced the gender binary as a means to divide and conquer. So no, trans* identities are not new; trans people were forced into hiding as fallout from imperialist methods of colonialism.

Conversations around coming out

If someone does come out to you, it is likely that they trust you with that information. They have chosen you as a safe space. However, just because you have been 'chosen', there could be other reasons, e.g. you may be the only person they *could* tell. For instance, there may have been a homophobic incident directed towards them in a class you teach. They may have to come out to you to explain what they experienced. Therefore, you have not been 'chosen' as a safe person, but you were the *necessary* person to tell in that situation. Either way, you have been trusted and therefore must be considerate with the information they have disclosed to you.

It is crucial to understand that for LGBTQ+ people, coming out is not a one-time occurrence. Queer people come out on multiple occasions across their lives. For some it gets easier, and for others it can feel just as daunting as the first time. Sharing your queerness still to this day can lead to negative responses, from indirect to direct discrimination, harassment, victimisation ... you name it, which thus adds weight to the importance of respecting and responding in a sensitive, informed way.

Unfortunately, we are living in a time when hate crimes directed against LGBTQ+ individuals are on the rise. While this chapter is not the place to discuss why this may be happening, it is important to keep yourself informed and updated as to what is happening in the current climate. External factors such as fear of being attacked all play into a queer person's day-to-day life. Being aware and open to learning about these stressors will make it easier for you to navigate these conversations.

Here are a few suggestions for how you could respond to someone who has come out to you as LGBTQ+.

First, it is always nice to thank the person for sharing, and to congratulate them.

'Thank you so much for sharing this with me, and congratulations for finding and being honest with who you are. I really admire you for stepping into your identity. And also, thank you for trusting me enough to share.'

'This might feel like a big question, but is there anything I can do to support you? What do you need from me?'

Especially if someone comes out as trans*, a welcomed response would be:

'Would you like me to use a different name or pronouns for you?'

For some, the answer will be yes. For others they might not be quite ready or sure yet. Either response from the person is valid. If the answer is 'yes':

'Yes actually, I would like to be called Amber and she/her pronouns please. Thank you.'

'Don't mention it. Anything I can do to support you! Are you comfortable with this when others are around? I just want to make sure I am not overstepping or accidentally outing you.'

'Maybe if we could keep it just us for now. My family don't know yet, but I am planning on telling them within the next couple of weeks. Thanks for checking.'

'So I presume if someone uses your old name, you don't want me to correct them? Yet, at least!'

'Yeah for the time being. I am not sure I am ready for people to know before my family.'

'Got it. It is a process, so you take the time you need and prioritise your safety and comfort! I'll practise, practise, practise! But from now on, you're Amber to me.'

'Thank you. It means a lot that you're going to try.'

Now this is a very formal conversation. In a more casual setting, it could be as simple as:

'So I've recently come to the realisation that I am a lesbian.'

'Oh wow, good for you for finding yourself!'

'Thanks – no one else knows so can we keep it on the down low?'

'Of course; you have my word. Thanks for sharing with me. You know I'm here if you want to talk anything out.'

'That's kind. Thank you.'

So, coming out doesn't have to be a *whole big thing!* While it can be big for that person, take into consideration what you already know about them. In the most casual words possible, assess the person's energy that they are bringing to the situation!

A beautiful example of a coming-out was in season two of the comedy drama *Feel Good*. A character is working out their gender identity. Their girlfriend simply replied:

'You let me know the words, and I will use them.'

It got me all choked up when I first watched it.

How to bring up identity

Say you have met with someone, and you are unsure about what pronouns to use for them; perhaps they look very androgynous. It is more than OK to ask someone how they would like to be referred to. As before, this does not have to be a formal conversation.

I would like to share an anecdote here. One time I was walking through the city centre, around 10:30pm. I bumped into a friend from university who was hanging out with people I had not met before. I was talking to one of the girls in the group and trying to help her book a taxi so she could get home safely. A little while into helping her, she turned to me and said:

'Cheeky pronoun check?'

Not only did this make me laugh, but it also made me realise that it is such a simple, simple thing to ask. So why do people avoid doing it?

When you (or others) get it 'wrong'

Oh no, you slipped up! It is OK; you are human at the end of the day. Humans are messy. The best way to deal with a genuine mistake is to correct yourself and move on. Sometimes apologising in the moment brings too much attention to the matter, especially when in a group setting. Instead, you can apologise afterwards to the person.

'I just wanted to apologise for deadnaming you earlier. I did correct myself afterwards and I promise I am trying. I will do better. Are you okay and can I do anything?'

Non-queer discussions on gender and sexuality

At the beginning of the chapter I noted how some conversations on gender and sexuality are not related to queer topics. So here are some other conversation topics that may arise.

The first is the most obvious – sex. Depending on the age range you work with or the field you are in, conversations around sex will vary greatly. It is important, no matter the age or situation, to hammer home the importance of consent. If you want to explore consent further, check out the website *The Art of Consent*, which has helpfully compiled many resources on consent (https://www.artofconsent.co.uk).

Talking about sexual health can feel taboo. Research suggests that many primary healthcare professionals find it difficult to discuss sexual topics and, as a result, the opportunities to prevent and intervene with risky sexual practices are missed (Skelton & Matthews, 2001), thereby showing the stigma around sexual health is deeply ingrained that even medical professionals are unable to fulfil their clinical duties (Ma & Loke, 2020).

Another example is BDSM (Bondage and Discipline, Dominance and Submission, Sadism and Masochism). BDSM is taboo, but you may be faced with conversations regarding this form of sexual practice. The research on BDSM is scarce, but what we do know is that in psychology, to build authentic connections with people, appropriate self-disclosure is required (Derlega & Grzelak, 1979). Narratives around BDSM are slowly changing. For example, the 'rough sex' defence is no longer recognised in UK courts. Despite this landmark progress, where BDSM is involved, there are many ways it can still go wrong. Therefore, if you are faced with disclosure around someone practising BDSM where something went 'wrong', it is important that you react with empathy and without judgement. The stigma around BDSM makes it harder for people to speak out. Adjacent to coming out as queer, as a trusted person it is your role to provide the individual with support and put your own prejudice to the side.

Curating a sex-positive environment will allow people to, firstly, feel more liberated and confident in their sexual choices, but also, it will give them the space to speak up about any concerns they may have.

Avoiding education burden

Education burden is the idea that the minoritised or marginalised group owe it to you to educate you on issues they face. While, yes, their voices are most important, it is also on you to do the work. Google is free! Sometimes a topic may come up that you do not know enough about, which is okay; it happens to us all. But it is then how you acknowledge this knowledge gap. You could say:

'Excuse my ignorance but could you briefly explain what that means so I have a better understanding?'

Or:

'I haven't heard about that but I will do some research so I can support you better.'

Rather than:

'What is that?'
  'This seems confusing.'
  'It's all a bit much these days.'

Yes, it might seem obvious, but I once had a actual pride organiser say that my pronouns confused her ... so it is good to cover all bases.

Intersectionality

There is no such thing as a single-issue struggle, because we do not live single-issue lives.

Audre Lorde

This quote by Audre Lorde sums it up perfectly. There is no one way to be gay. No one experience of being gay. There is no one way to be non-binary. No single experience of being non-binary. No one way to be Black. No single experience of being Black. No one way to be autistic. No single experience of being autistic. You get it. Every facet of our identity interacts and will be deeply personal to our own lived experience. This is something to consider when talking about gender and sexuality. For example, discussions around safe sex practices must acknowledge younger people, those of lower socio-economic status, and those who misuse alcohol and other drugs as being more likely to engage in risky sexual behaviours (Department of Health, 2013; NICE, 2007; Royal College of Physicians, 2011; Hogben & Leichliter, 2008). By only acknowledging the behaviour of risky sexual practices, it can take away from this person's intersectional experience. Of course, it can be more complex than this. No one is expecting you to have a full competency around all social issues related to gender and sexuality; instead, it will benefit you to engage with the whole person.

Steps you can take

Signalling

Research by Heath and Mulligan (2007) has shown that some non-heterosexual women will not correct their health practitioners if they are making incorrect assumptions about them. Maybe a doctor refers to the patient's husband rather than the patient's wife. It was found that they would only correct the practitioner if they felt it was safe to do so. It may seem cliched, but you can signal your LGBTQ+ allyship so that those you work with feel able to disclose their identity and be their authentic self around you. This can be done by displaying a rainbow sticker, a mini pride flag, including that you are an ally in your email signature, or even LGBTQ+ inclusive posters. Oftentimes people would interpret this behaviour as tokenistic, but for queer individuals navigating a new environment or meeting a new practitioner, they will feel able to be their authentic self with you. In turn, a better client–practitioner relationship can be established.

Another simple display of allyship is including your own pronouns in your email signature. Many cisgender people do not feel the need to do this as it 'doesn't apply to them'. However, by doing so, it is showing LGBTQ+ individuals and other allies that this is something you have considered, Also, for those of you who have gender-neutral names, this can be helpful for communicating with people who have not met you before. I have they/she in my email signature and in my module handbooks, so students know how to address me from the beginning of the semester. Some do not know what this means, so it opens up the conversation for them to ask how to best address me or talk about me. It is good practice. I also have a pronoun badge on my lanyard, and students have asked where they can get their own – yet again a simple signal of acceptance and inclusion.

Validation

As we have explored in this chapter, queer people face barriers that those who are cisgender and heterosexual do not. Therefore, in your role, be it a teacher, nurse, social worker, or educator, you can contribute to the positive well-being of queer people by simply recognising the impact of queer discrimination and how this can link to high-risk behaviours and poor mental health outcomes (Lee et al., 2016).

Example
'My mum has not really communicated with me recently. I think we have become distant since I came out to her.'
Non-validating
'We all have issues with parents!'
Validating
'Dealing with parents can be so tricky. I can only imagine how much harder it must be when they don't accept you for who you are.'

Just by choosing your words slightly more carefully, you are helping to validate and affirm the person's identity.

Challenge your own prejudices

We all hold prejudices, some more overt than others. It is important for us to be aware of these biases we hold. By acknowledging our biases, we can start to do better. If you happen to be called out for your biases, try not to be defensive. Instead, it is best to take it as a learning opportunity. By no means is this an easy act; it takes time, effort, and, most importantly, your own motivation to want to do better. I encourage you to enjoy the challenge.

Active allyship

All of the above, in fact the majority of this chapter, are forms of active allyship. To classify as an ally, you also need to advocate for the rights of LGBTQ+ individuals outside of their presence. Yes, this does mean having some difficult conversations, potentially with those very dear to you, but luckily you have a book in your hand that should help make that process more manageable. Being an ally is a journey, and it can be a fun one. Once you open yourself up to different identities and life experiences, life becomes more colourful – trust me.

Time to put your knowledge into practice. Consider the following three scenarios and answer the prompts for each of them. You can adjust the context to something more applicable to you, but the principles will remain.

Case study 1: Spoken

You are a social worker. A family you work with has had heightened tensions recently. You discover that their middle child Rhys (aged 12) has come out as a transgender boy. Rhys has asked to not be referred to as his deadname, Amelia, and would like to be referred to with he/him pronouns. The mum has not taken the news well. The dad is accepting but doesn't quite get it. They've asked Rhys to keep it a secret from his other two siblings and extended family and friends. The mum continues to buy Rhys girly clothes and refer to him as Amelia and her 'little girl'. The mum shares with you that she thinks it is just a fad and 'she's too young to understand'. She is also concerned that Rhys has been 'groomed' into this lifestyle. Rhys has been acting out at home and has become increasingly withdrawn and quiet over the last two years. Rhys is not ready to discuss this with you, but he has told you that he is very unhappy and that his parents don't care for him.

How would you navigate this conversation with Rhys' parents? How would you show your support for Rhys? Do you feel confident addressing this situation? How can you ensure the conversation remains non-confrontational?

Suggested responses

To Parents:

'I understand this is a challenging and unexpected situation, and it's okay to feel uncertain. Many young people like Rhys start to recognise their true gender identity around this age – it's a deeply felt sense of who they are, not something they have been "groomed" into. Research shows that affirming a child's gender identity can significantly improve their well-being. As we know, Rhys has been acting out and withdrawing. This is likely to be because he is feeling distressed. What he needs most right now is your love and support. As a first step, you might consider using the name Rhys rather than Amelia and using male pronouns at home. This might feel different at first, but it could make a big difference in how supported he feels.

'There are excellent resources and support groups for parents in your situation, and I'm here to provide materials and guidance whenever you're ready. This will be a journey for your family, and I'm here to support you every step of the way to ensure Rhys feels safe and loved.'

To Rhys:

'I know you may not be ready to talk about your identity, and that's okay – there's no pressure. Just know that I'm here for you whenever you're ready. In the meantime, if you would prefer me to use a different name or pronouns for you, let me know. It's okay to feel different; who you are is valid, and I'm here to support you.'

It is important to note here that Rhys is not ready to talk about his identity. Remaining vague would be more beneficial than enforcing complex conversations around gender identity. These responses allow space for Rhys to share as much or as little as he wants.

Case study 2: Written

You are a head teacher at an academy trust school in a rural area.

Across year groups in your school, there has been a sudden increase in anti-LGBTQ+ views and incidents. Despite your best efforts to show solidarity to the LGBTQ+ community, e.g. LGBTQ+ History Month, student pride network, the hateful rhetoric persists. Parents are becoming increasingly concerned about their children's welfare, especially after an incident where a Year 8 boy was beaten up in the boy's changing rooms for being 'perceived' as gay.

How would you issue a statement on this incident? What fallout would you need to consider from doing so? How would you support the victimised student and their family?

A whole school communication should be distributed to parents, students, and the teachers stressing zero tolerance of homophobia and transphobia. The communication should also outline the school's protocol if incidents occur, e.g. isolation, detention, mandatory PSHE. The perpetrator(s) could also have a direct educational intervention – whatever that may look like from the school. The school should also commit to further education on LGBTQ+ rights and providing a safe space for LGBTQ+ students. Parental meetings and regular contact with the parents of the child who was victim to this incident should be organised.

Case study 3: Online

You are a secondary school teacher.

You received a text from a colleague saying that they won't be coming into work today due to being the victim of a homophobic incident from another colleague the day prior. She shares that no one knows that it happened. You do not know her very well, but you do know that this colleague has recently come out as lesbian.

How would you respond to this text? What would you do? Would you elevate this, and if so, how?

Suggested response

'Hey, I'm really sorry to hear this and it is not okay that this has happened to you, especially at work. Do you want to talk it out with me? I am happy to escalate this, as it unacceptable. I know we don't know each other very well, but I am in your corner 100%. Let me know and look after yourself.'

You may feel uncomfortable escalating this incident without her consent; however, this should be seen as a safeguarding concern. Therefore, it would be best practice to report it to the appropriate lead (e.g., headteacher) without giving identifiable details of either party. It will then be in the hands of your school to deal with the incident – this will differ depending on the school's policy and workplace culture. You should also familiarise yourself with the school's equality, diversity, and inclusion policies to ensure the right steps are taken.

Conclusion

Reading this chapter is not going to make you the beacon of all things queer or all things related to gender and sexuality. Even as a queer individual who has been out since the age of 15, I am still learning every single day. Being an LGBTQ+ ally requires work and constant education on the pressing issues the community faces. Only by being aware of the current climate will your communication with LGBTQ+ individuals be enhanced. By taking these steps, you are making the world a safer place for queer individuals, especially queer youth who are growing up amidst harmful rhetoric.

Key takeaways

- Someone's gender/sexuality is only one part of that person. Above being queer, there will be hundreds of other incredible facets of that person. They are still the person you knew before they came out – don't make being queer the focal point of all conversations going forwards
- Have conversations in your workplace to identify how you can all be more accommodating to LGBTQ+ people. Maybe it is as simple as updating your intake forms, or maybe you all need to engage with an LGBTQ+ awareness programme. All efforts are good efforts!
- Conversations on gender and sexuality are not always queer. Sex-positivity can liberate everyone to be more open about sexual health and practice
- Stay in the loop about current policy and social issues that certain identities might be facing so that you can support individuals in your role as a professional or friend while being informed of the extra stressors they might be facing
- Keep challenging yourself and commit to being an active ally so that you can navigate these difficult conversations with more confidence and nuance.

References

Cameron, J.J., & Stinson, D.A. (2019). Gender (mis)measurement: Guidelines for respecting gender diversity in psychological research. *Social and Personality Psychology Compass, 13*(11), e12506.

Department of Health. (2013). A framework for sexual health improvement in England. https://assets.publishing.service.gov.uk/media/5a7aba03e5274a34770e6b 1e/9287-2900714-TSO-SexualHealthPolicyNW_ACCESSIBLE.pdf.

Derlega, V.J., & Grzelak, J. (1979). Appropriateness of self-disclosure. In G. Chelune (Ed.), *Self-disclosure: Origins, patterns, and implications of openness in interpersonal relationships*. San Francisco, CA: Jossey-Bass.

Fausto-Sterling, A. (1993). The five sexes. *The Sciences* (March/April), 20–25.

Heath, M., & Mulligan, E. (2007). Seeking open minded doctors – how women who identify as bisexual, queer or lesbian seek quality health care. *Australian Family Physician, 36*(6).

Hogben, M., & Leichliter, J.S. (2008). Social determinants and sexually transmitted disease disparities. *Sexually Transmitted Diseases, 35*, S13–S18.

Home Office. (2023). Hate crime, England and Wales, 2022 to 2023 second edition. https:// www.gov.uk/government/statistics/hate-crime-england-and-wales-2022-to-2023/ hate-crime-england-and-wales-2022-to-2023.

Index on Censorship. (2024). Banned: School librarians shushed over LGBT+ books. https://www.indexoncensorship.org/2024/08/banned-school-librarians-shushed- over-lgbt-books/.

Joel, D. (2021). Beyond the binary: Rethinking sex and the brain. *Neuroscience & Biobehavioral Reviews, 122*, 165–175.

Lee, J.H., Gamarel, K.E., Bryant, K.J., Zaller, N.D., & Operario, D. (2016). Discrimination, mental health, and substance use disorders among sexual minority populations. *LGBT Health, 3*(4), 258–265.

Ma, H., & Loke, A.Y. (2020). A scoping review of an HIV/AIDS-related stigma-reduction intervention for professionals and students from health-related disciplines. *International Journal of Sexual Health, 32*(2), 94–129.

National Institute for Health and Clinical Excellence (NICE). (2017). *One to one interventions to reduce the transmission of sexually transmitted infections (STIs) including HIV, and to reduce the rate of under 18 conceptions, especially among vulnerable and at risk groups*. NICE public health guidance 3. London: NICE.

Royal College of Physicians. (2011). *Alcohol and sex: A cocktail for poor sexual health. A report of the Alcohol and Sexual Health Working Party*. London: Royal College of Physicians.

Skelton, J.R., & Matthews, P.M. (2001). Teaching sexual history taking to health care professionals in primary care. *Medical education, 35*(6), 603–608.

United Nations Free & Equal. (n.d.). Intersex people. https://unfe.org/en/know-the-facts/challenges-solutions/intersex.

10

Uncomfortable conversations about race

Mia Edwards

Introduction

This chapter addresses tensions inherent to many conversations about race, exploring how the discomfort so often rife in such discussions can be tackled, alleviated, and learned from. This work benefits our understanding and communication of issues around race and creates progress towards a truly anti-racist society.

The techniques I share here are for anyone: for fellow people of colour (POCs) and White allies. They are for the exhausted and for the invigorated; for the enraged and the curious. I'll explore the tools that we can refine and adapt at our own discretion when navigating everyday complexity and conflict.

What is racial justice?

To begin, let's study the cultural and political discourse encapsulating and informing tensions underlying misunderstandings around racial justice. This is a key point to evaluate, given that it underlies much of what we disagree on. What *is* racial justice?

Well, we haven't collectively decided yet. In March 2024 a conversation unravelled between then-Prime Minister Rishi Sunak – who is of Indian Punjabi descent – and Black writer of the controversial play *Slave Play*[1] Jeremy O. Harris. Harris, a writer and actor, scribed the play to interrogate the complex interaction between colonialism and sex.

I watched the play with a White friend. As a POC, I was enthralled by its unpacking of how colonial forces still burden our ability to share sexual and emotional joy in partnership with White people, since this exchange feels at odds with the world we inherit. But I winced after watching with my well-meaning friend – rightfully eager as she was to learn about psychosexual

DOI: 10.4324/9781003433248-13

racial dynamics from those best-versed in it – when the inevitable uncomfortable pause between us arose after curtain fall. I had enough to process after watching the stark unpacking of my reality without the instinctive responsibility I felt for stepping around her discomfort.

Harris understood this discomfort. Within the play's 13-week London run, he incorporated two nights open exclusively to those identifying as Black – 'Black Out Nights' – to allow racially minoritised viewers to watch the performance 'free from the white gaze' (Walker, 2024, writing in the *Guardian*).

In explanation, Harris shared that 'in most places in the West, poor people and Black people have been told that they do not belong inside of the theatre … [so] it is a necessity to radically invite them in with initiatives that say, *'you're* invited – specifically *you*' (BBC Sounds, 2024).

When asked whether it was discriminatory to actively *un*invite White people to showings – even if Black Out Nights comprised only around 2% of total performances (Akbar, 2024, writing in the *Guardian*) – he rebutted, saying that the many White-dominated spaces in the global North were not being scrutinised for their historic exclusivity, despite blatant racial discrepancies (BBC Sounds, 2024).

Theatres are a convenient example of what he was referring to. According to Arts Council England's research, in 2020–2021, just 7% of its audiences for organisations under its National Portfolio identified as being ethnically 'Mixed', 'Asian or Asian British', 'Black or Black British', or 'Other' (Arts Council England, 2021). How else to dent a 93% White majority of theatre audiences than 'radically' inviting those who felt barred from the party? There's no banner on theatre websites uninviting certain demographics; some banners aren't so explicit.

Nonetheless, political uproar ensued. Sunak's representative declared the inclusion of Black Out Nights 'concerning', clarifying that the Prime Minister was 'a big supporter of the arts and he believes that the arts should be inclusive and open to everyone, particularly where those arts venues are in receipt of public funding'. Moreover, the representative declared, 'restricting audiences on the basis of race would be wrong and divisive' (Walker, 2014, writing in the *Guardian*).

Wrong and divisive. Persuasive and absolute adjectives, lacking real substance or meaning – key components of rhetoric. The representative's reference to public funding is cheeky given the ways racially minoritised groups were disadvantaged by the Conservative Party's austerity measures, structuring of the prison estate, and scapegoating of migrants (United Nations, 2019). As for divisiveness, is it more divisive to publicly decry an attempt to counter disproportionality in the arts, or to attempt to counter disproportionality in the arts? I'd hazard a guess at the former.

Irrespective, this exchange exemplifies the multifaceted and often antagonistic tensions informing many discussions on race. Let's unpack what the fundamental disagreement was here – and see what lessons are hidden in the conflict.

Racial equity vs racial equality

In the example given in the last section, both partakers in the discussion – Sunak and Harris – are people of colour, but they promote contrasting notions of justice.

Equity means distributing resources according to need, ensuring that everyone can access the same opportunities and prospects irrespective of difference; some groups receive more resources than others, to compensate for a comparative deficit of such resources (Hansson, 2001). My reading of Harris' argument is that this is the model of justice that he promotes: by actively inviting racially minoritised groups to a performance, he addresses the *disinvitation* that these groups receive implicitly through the reproduction of institutional 'Whiteness-as-norm' (Winings, 2019).

Conversely, equality means allotting identical resources and opportunities to everyone, irrespective of variations in socioeconomic and racial privilege and advantage (Hansson, 2001). In pushing for everyone to have the same access to *Slave Play*, Sunak argues for this model in which no demographic is given precedence over another.

Let's explore the 'deficit' shouldered by non-White people that Harris attempts to counter by advocating for Black Out Nights. Reviewing race through a lens of *fundamental inequity* helps us to understand race as a concept moulded around Whiteness-as-norm, and non-Whiteness as a surplus; there is inequity inherent to this existential imbalance. The concept of race depends on a notion of the 'Other' – in that when we refer to race, we really refer to how people veer from Whiteness (Ahmed, 2007).

White and non-White people do not have parity of experience. Centuries of colonial history can impede the most minute interactions to the socioeconomic conditions of POCs due to our race. Many of us harbour a chronic awareness of where we stand in relation to Whiteness – something that most White people could never conceptualise or embody (Fanon, 1952). White people are gifted spaces moulded to convene and reinforce their reality as existential norm; a model of equity would mean that, at the very least, progress is made to counter this.

From an equity perspective, Black Out Nights are a valuable start for relinquishing Whiteness-as-norm, creating spaces that make progress in ensuring that everyone carries their fair share of cultural and political value.

As for Sunak (admittedly a powerful billionaire – so not necessarily someone particularly disadvantaged by the global racial hegemony), his point might reflect his catering to the prevailing political interests of his party and voters. Someone for whom racial justice means racial equity might argue that advocating for racial equality could demonstrate an attempt to supersede the inequities inherent to POCs' existence by leaning into the political, economic, and cultural traditions passed down by the coloniser, thus drawing them closer to the power associated with a political conception of Whiteness (Mitchell, 2022).

If Sunak had said, for example, 'whilst I understand that there is racial disproportionality in participation with, and consumption of, the arts, I advocate for a system in which everyone has equal access to insightful art, from which those of all races have much to learn', the conversation might have felt more civilised and less like an attempt to intentionally enrage and divide to appease political supporters (ironically, the accusation he held against Harris). There are two takeaways for conversationalists here:

- POCs often experience the inner conflict of grappling with their own identities, which stand in contrast with the rhetoric-riddled, simplistic statements made by those who reap the political benefits of division. Bear this in mind when speaking to POCs about our own reality, taking note of whether your perspective has been shaped by institutional narratives that do not centre on lived experience. Arguments of equity vs equality risk erasing the excess psychological baggage that people of colour carry.
- Uncomfortable conversations can be an opportunity to listen. If Sunak really cared about championing the particularities of living as a POC, perhaps he would have deigned to simply listen to the discussion unfold, instead of dismissing it. Sometimes, it's enough to just sit and absorb someone's explanation. Being anti-racist involves researching and listening – and even people of colour can learn from other POCs about the complexities of racial injustice, and how to counter them.

Racism in education

My experience of education in the UK demonstrates many of the themes that are relevant to this chapter. I will begin with an incident that occurred a few years ago but will probably be familiar to many young people.

When I was studying GCSE Child Development, the teacher handed out plastic babies for us as part of a class project. In line with the classroom demographic, all babies were White – bar one. The most gobby girl (let's call her Gobby) in the class was the recipient of the darker baby, which had my South Asian hues. 'Ew, I don't want that one!' exclaimed Gobby. 'It's a Paki!'

The entire classroom turned to look at me – the resident Paki – and winced. The (White) teacher looked to Gobby, then to me, sheepish. 'Gobby', she said with humoured exasperation.

Then that's it. That's all that happened. We moved on.

I'd observe that Gobby held none of the tension arising from her comment; she got confidently on with her remarking. The teacher held some of the tension – wanting to navigate appeasing her favourite pupil while side-eyeing me to relegate any guilt at not imposing any consequences for Gobby's actions. But who was forced to hold almost all the actual tension? The awkwardness of others? The lack of accountability or consolidation? The normalisation? Not the teacher; not Gobby; not my White classmates.

As children, POCs are thrust into our racialised realities, tasked with correcting others or making the decision to be silent where a fight is too exhausting or too futile.

But this conversation needn't have been so unpleasant. If traversed healthily, educational institutions can allow for educators to be meaningful mediators; for those conditioned into racism to have their assumptions challenged; for children of colour to learn that they do not have to be Othered, silenced, allotted the task of 'peacekeeper' to divert the discomfort of others.

Pupils pick up a great deal from the (perceived) adult in the room. This process is beautifully encapsulated by Palmer in this passage from *The Courage to Teach* (1998):

> I project the conditions of my soul onto my students ... and our way of being together ... If I am willing to look in that mirror and not run from what I see, I have a chance to gain self-knowledge ... and knowing myself is as crucial to good teaching as knowing my students and my subject (49).

If the classroom mimics the teacher's inner world, what does the lone pupil of colour represent to the teacher ill at ease with themselves? The likelihood is that they represent the part of the teacher that is ashamed – the part that dares not show its face. Conversely, the popular White student likely represents the teacher that can more comfortably reveal itself; the part that must be appeased to avoid being shunned.

Much of the projection of a rejectable Other reflects our own self-shame (Fanon, 1952). Without countering this, educators risk replicating their own understanding of the world and themselves in the classroom. What were my peers picking up about what children of colour could legitimately represent to them from the actions of this particular trusted adult? Likely the POCs were figures whom they could acceptably marginalise to maintain the status quo that kept their accepted self – Whiteness-as-norm – on top.

Let's review how the conversation could have gone differently. There are three facets through which the conversation's direction could have been changed to be productive and anti-racist.

Racism and shame

First, the teacher's internalised shame manifesting as racist complicity must be reflected on. Practitioners of any race should ensure that their internalised racism is acknowledged and addressed to avoid this inner conflict playing out in the classroom.

Anti-racism must be nourished via personal research to counter lifelong exposure to racist signalling. Self-reflection and anti-racism is best done in the therapy room, with a trained professional (many of whom also have a particular specialism in anti-racism). Were this personal work to have taken place prior to this altercation, the teacher could have followed – and not repressed – the alarm alerting her to respond to the racism. She could have enacted a structured follow-up instead of being led by her fear of rejection.

Authentic anti-racism can only occur alongside an addressing of self (Zembylas, 2022). Lacking the assuredness to hold our own makes it more difficult to defy classroom behaviour that risks making us unpopular with pupils: such inaction means that it falls on global majority children to do the correcting themselves.

Assuredly calling out classroom racism might look like this:

'Gobby, it makes me very sad that you would use words that are so hateful and racist – and that's just me as a White person who cannot possibly experience what girls of colour in this classroom might be feeling.'

Centring

Interestingly, when being 'noticed' during racist incidents (which occurred as the whole classroom turned to look at me at the utterance of the racial slur), what racially minoritised children experience is *decentring*. A perfect example of this is shared in former primary teacher Darren Chetty's essay (2016: 96), outlining that when a boy in his class hailing from Nigeria wrote and shared a story with the class about a member of his family, he was interrupted by a classmate who identified as being from the Congo. 'You can't say that! Stories have to be about White people', was his classmate's interjection.

Inequalities experienced in the classroom shape what children expect and understand of the world (Collins, 2009). If global majority children are chronically framed as interlopers on our peers' culturally dominant and accepted stories, we do not know to honour ourselves in esteem, wonder, and imagination – experiences that should be fundamental childhood pillars. POCs instead come to represent the blemish that can merely accompany White stories. That's why it's so integral that we hail classrooms – rare spaces in which different viewpoints and experiences are united at a point when our worldview is still forming – as opportunities to decentre Whiteness via uncomfortable conversations (Linton & Dei, 2019).

Once 'Paki' was floated, I was inevitably lit up LED-style to my peers. Educators should not pretend that the pupil of colour hasn't been noticed, but instead aim to control the direction of this noticing. To achieve this, the teacher could say something like this:

'The people of colour in this room are very important, and very welcome here – in fact, when studying child development, it's them we can learn from because they probably understand better than anyone the ways that children's development can be shaped by harmful narratives about race. Gobby, please stay behind at the end of the lesson; I'm interested in discussing why you chose to use that word.'

This narrative appropriately signposts to the class that something is amiss, raising the alarm for the class's subconscious acknowledging of the importance of responding to racism. It also doesn't negate the focus on people of colour, but acknowledges the disproportionate impact of the conversation on them and emphasises the constructive contribution they could make *as a result of their inherent understanding of racism*. It subverts the centring/decentring from a negative to a positive one, averting racial sidelining by giving POCs a 'starring' role in their classroom story.

Likewise, it removes responsibility from the POC to the teacher for addressing racism, and prevents the POC from having to be exposed to any racist outbursts that might come from Gobby in the unpicking process. The teacher is clarifying: it is *my* responsibility to hold this discomfort, and any collateral that you are taking on as a result is not fair, and I'm sorry.

Making space

Mindfulness is a tool that can be practised and harnessed to enhance awareness of self (mind and body) amongst students (Hanh & Weare, 2017). Mindful practice can involve focusing on one's breath and physical sensations to enhance help promote clarity of thought.

The role of an educator should be to harness children's growth, so that their pupils' psyches supersede the barriers afflicting previous generations; mindfulness can be a very helpful tool to this end.

When teachers avoid acknowledging and addressing racism, it teaches White children not to notice racism, and non-White children to pretend not to notice it. Glossing over the moment risks missing the nuance of what quietly entrenches racism.

Allowing the class to experience and lean into discomfort via a mindful check-in following a racist incident shows immense self-confidence. It demonstrates an ability to address things as they are – even when things are complicated. It also helps young people to acknowledge the fear, grief, or hysteria that they might all – irrespective of their colour – be feeling when racism occurs, facilitating a process of unpacking and reflection (Anālayo, 2020).

Introducing this mindful pause could look something like this:

'I'd like to sit with what was just said before moving on with the lesson. How are we doing? Shall we sit with our breath for a moment, feel the pressure of the chair on our body, and tune in to how we are feeling?'

This represents a collective acknowledgement of the circumstances – allowing those in the room to *notice and process* what has happened – and makes room for reflection and learning.

Challenging racists

Case study: Arguing with racists

This segment won't focus on the outcomes of arguing with a racist, but rather how we might engage in productive discussion with them. We are responsible for challenging racism, but we are not at fault if we can't change the mind of a racist. The cause of someone's racism may well be beyond our control.

I have been lucky enough to travel the world, during which I have witnessed varying attitudes towards those from different races and cultures – some of them refreshing, some of them concerning. A less positive example was revealed when I was sitting in a café in a Colombian mountainside town, where a White Canadian man sat beside me and engaged me in animated conversation.

He commenced by complaining that the COVID-19 lockdowns were unfair on racially minoritised groups in 'developing' countries because the shutdown of labour prevented these groups from working in industries like tourism – sectors on which many of them depended to keep financially afloat.

If the welfare of minoritised groups was his biggest concern, wouldn't his focus be on their ability to shelter from COVID-19 and continue to receive financial support, thereby being protected from the pandemic's harms? In other words, if he really cared about justice for minoritised groups, wouldn't he advocate to change the international power balance so that their well-being was valued equally with those in the global North where these privileges were more often afforded? Instead, his real complaint was the hindrance that the pandemic posed to his capacity to jet around and be sufficiently served by those whom the world economic order decreed as his financial servant.

He was talking about maintaining his privilege in a world of Whiteness-as-norm.

My suspicion of his racism was reinforced by his next rant:

'It's ridiculous that BAME people are given skilled jobs – for example, in medicine and law – over White people who have attended the good schools (the institutions that really prepare people for those roles) – just because of the "disadvantaged/race" card. Some people are primed for these jobs, and BAME people are just being handed them over a sob story.'

'It's unfair that I, as a consumer, suffer as a result of receiving less sophisti-cated service from underqualified health professionals just to appease these diversity quotas.'

So many fallacies: that the drive and intellect to excel in competitive roles is contingent upon the resources one receives in accordance with one's socioeconomic standing; that all POCs in Canada are necessarily poor; that certain groups can access such specialist roles without undergoing appropri-ate training.

All of this said to me, a relatively middle-class, clearly educated Tamil woman, apparently some POCs don't spend fraught childhoods in deep pov-erty, plotting to overthrow White would-be doctors. Who knew?

When POCs 'infiltrate' and achieve in spaces in which Whiteness has been reinforced as the cultural and economic dominator, white supremacists have a problem: the fear and insecurity that they've countered by categoris-ing a perceived Other as aggressor or imbecile, and themselves as a victim of this 'violence' or stupidity, risks no longer being justified (Kinnvall & Merino, 2023). To maintain the superiority schema, white supremacists still seek to justify their defensive entitlement even when it becomes clear that racially minoritised communities have the same innate abilities as White people (as demonstrated in this case study, with the man's implication being that 'the only reason for the Other to professionally progress at the historic level of White people is because they have an unfair advantage sustained through manipulation of "victim status"'). That way, the white supremacist's sense of being 'unfairly' disadvantaged, by the elevated attainment of the Other in a system that otherwise neatly privileges them, is maintained.

Someone who subscribes to an unsound argument – an argument lacking true premises (Vorobej, 2006) – will not be swayed by a case constructed via rational deduction, because rational deduction is not their valued mecha-nism for belief-building.

Rational argument with irrational arguers is futile; you'll be doomed to incite the emotion underlying their irrational beliefs (Singpurwalla, 2006), wasting time and capacity.

Using Socratic questioning

So how to rebut?

Enter Socratic questioning. This technique is effective at getting people – even the irrational – to assess their own thought processes; it's also possible to use even when you're feeling too stunned, fatigued, or furious for the moral battleground. It involves impartial questioning to stimulate critical thinking, diverting from the rhetoric that poisons much racial discourse.

First off, it involves receiving, reflecting, and summarising (Paul & Elder, 2007). This can entail painful listening if you're literally paying attention (as I was) to someone explain why you are less intelligent and worthy of professional development than they are. But it does help to avoid the interrogatory figure – in this instance, me – being demonised or easily used as 'see what I mean! You're all the same! You people won't even let me get a word in!' scapegoat, since it removes the need for you to express your opinion at all.

A sidenote to POCs: there's no pressure on you to engage with such conversations. Productive discussions are to be had if you have the energy and capacity to defend your right to exist on a par with others. No judgement if you'd rather give them the finger and get on with your day.

But presuming we do have the energy to continue with the conversation, let's use this case study as a basis for this method's implication. I focused on one of his claims:

'BAME people are given skilled jobs … just because of the "disadvantage/ race" card.'

'Interesting', I responded. *'Can I ask what you mean by the "race card"?'*

'The race card is a tactic used by these people to access higher-paid roles without having the credibility to actually do them well.'

'It sounds like you feel as though some people are less qualified than others to do the jobs that society puts a lot of value on but are given the job nonetheless.'

This is the reflecting and paraphrasing – I *hear* you. I'm listening.

'Yep.'

'You've used the word credibility – could you define that?'

'Sure – it means how qualified you are for a job.'

'Ah, I see. The thing is, I thought there were specific exams everyone has to pass to qualify for roles like being a doctor or lawyer, no matter what their education or upbringing looked like.'

'Right. But to get to those exams I mean.'

'Ah OK, so you feel that to be given the opportunity to even get to a point where people can compete for those jobs, some groups have an advantage.'

'Right.'

'Could we delve deeper into what you mean by "advantage"?'

And so on. When employing this method, you can conduct an almost clinical inquisition that incites a critical thinking approach to expose the fallacies in their reasoning and makes them reassess the validity of their original claim. I could then go on to raise the contradiction in his idea of 'advantage' compared with the inherent disadvantages that he'd previously insisted BAME groups have in a capitalist system. Which are we, advantaged or disadvantaged? Your points are muddled and sweeping.

The goal of this technique is to change your conversational partner's mind. There were specific areas that I wanted him to identify and consider by the end of the conversation. First up was his motivation for having his views in the first place:

'The foundations of my views about the perceived advantage of racially minoritised groups are informed by my feelings towards them and towards myself, and not by fact.'

Secondly, and more complicated to do, I wanted him to identify how much of his flawed logic was to protect him from having to confront his own discriminatory instinct:

'Whilst I claim that I am not racist, I extract my moral rationale from a capitalistic framework that dictates that some people are less worthy of professional and economic value – arguably of much value at all within a capitalist system – than others.'

'I cannot justify my support for this system – instead, I extract all of my reasoning from within the confines of this system so that I essentially present the system as being self-justifying.'

'I know that this system explicitly disadvantages others and privileges me, but I still advocate for it as I believe that White people possess an inherent right

to success – and even an elevated intelligence – over people of colour, which is my real, unspoken justification for my support of this system.'

'I am a racist.'

Ambitious, yes. Worth a shot though.

Note the calm and passive questioning; you're encouraging the other person to interrogate their own views, validating them by paraphrasing their own points back to them. You're intentionally avoiding antagonistic prodding (Paul & Elder, 2019). Given that premises of unsound arguments are often based on assumptions or feelings as opposed to facts, this inquiry can help illuminate to someone the fallacies foundational to their reasoning.

I'll never know whether I changed a mind that day; I hope, at the very least, I stimulated productive self-interrogation in someone whose views denied full global majority personhood.

'So if you walked into the doctor's office', I asked, in a final attempt to expose his own racism to him, *'and I called you in to my office – because, in this example, I am your doctor – would you assume that I would be incapable of providing you with a good medical service because I am less intelligent than a White doctor would be?'*

'It's getting that way, yes', he confidently concurred.

Had I the energy, I would have asked him to define intelligence – is it innate or not innate? If you're suggesting that I'm less intelligent because of my colour, can you really claim that you are not a racist?

At least, he had admitted his own prejudice, his racism peeking through the mask of 'it's not me, it's just the system!' A small victory.

But by this point, I was tired.

I calmly delivered my first opinion of the two-hour conversation:

'As a – by the way, very intelligent – brown woman, I'd like to suggest that you follow your instinct and refuse service from racially minoritised people. We don't want to waste our valuable wisdom on those who believe that we aren't capable of such intellect. Nice to meet you; have a good day.'

Conclusion

Understanding the complex nature of social justice can help you to be more rational or critical in your understanding of the different forces that impact people's perception of what true justice means, and be more strategic in your communication around racial issues. When we lack the confidence to challenge racism, it can be because we lack the confidence to go against the grain – which relates to self-shame. Not many people would admit to their own racism, but racism is structurally ingrained and dwells in us all. Authentic anti-racism is best practised when our moral responsibility and drive to speak out is coupled with our confidence to insert ourselves in a space that might make others bristle. By using neutral conversations to combat racism, the antagonism that draws racists into a space of contempt can be avoided and flawed perceptions challenged. Conversations about race may be uncomfortable but they are essential if the cycle of racist normalisation is ever to be broken.

Key takeaways

- Understand political, economic and cultural complexities in narratives around racial justice
- Acknowledge instances of racism, instead of letting them slide
- Use mindfulness as a technique for processing following racist incidents
- Work on your own self-shame and racism
- Combat racism with neutral interrogation

Note

1 The official page of the play's London run can be found here: https://www.noelcowardtheatre.co.uk/whats-on/slave-play.

References

Ahmed, S. (2007). A phenomenology of Whiteness. *Feminist Theory, 8*(2), 149–168.

Akbar, A. (2024). Sunak's sabre-rattling is pure cynicism – Black Out Nights are a small, vital corrective to theatre's lack of diversity. *Guardian*, 4 March. https://www.theguardian.com/commentisfree/2024/mar/04/rishi-sunak-black-out-nights-theatre-diversity-slave-play.

Anālayo, B. (2020). Confronting racism with mindfulness. *Mindfulness, 11*, 2283–2297.

Armistead, C. (2024). 'White supremacy was never hidden from me': Jeremy O. Harris on bringing Broadway hit Slave Play to the UK. *Guardian*, 9 June. https://www.theguardian.com/stage/article/2024/jun/09/jeremy-o-harris-slave-play-broadway-london-colonialism.

Arts Council England. (2021). *Equality, diversity and inclusion: A Data Report.*

BBC Sounds. (2024). *Slave Play to host all-black audience nights* [Podcast], 27 February. https://www.bbc.co.uk/sounds/play/p0hfc4yv.

Chetty, D. (2016). You can't say that! Stories have to be about White people! In N. Shukla (Ed.), *The good immigrant* (pp. 96–108). London: Penguin Books.

Collins, J. (2009). Social reproduction in classrooms and schools. *Annual Review of Anthropology, 38*, 33–48.

Fanon, F. (1952). *Black skin, White masks.* New York: Grove Press.

Hanh, T.N., & Weare, K. (2017). *Happy teachers change the world.* Berkeley, CA: Parallax Press.

Hansson, S.O. (2001). Equity, equality, and egalitarianism. *Archives for Philosophy of Law and Social Philosophy, 87*(4), 529–541.

Kinnvall, C., & Merino, P.K. (2023). Deglobalization and the political psychology of white supremacy. *Theory & Psychology, 33*(2), 227–248.

Linton, R., & Dei, G.J.S. (2019). Racism in schools and classrooms: Towards an anti-racist pedagogy of power and systemic privilege. In A. Jule (Ed.), *The Compassionate Educator* (pp. 271–293). Toronto: Canadian Scholars.

Mitchell, J. (2022). Back to race, not beyond race: Multiraciality and racial identity in the United States and Brazil. *Comparative Migrant Studies, 10*(22), 1–22.

Palmer, P.J. (1998). *The courage to teach: Exploring the inner landscape of a teacher's life.* Hoboken, NJ: Jossey-Bass.

Paul, R., & Elder, L. (2007). Critical thinking: The art of Socratic questioning. *Journal of Developmental Education, 31*(1), 36–37.

Paul, R., & Elder, L. (2019). *The thinker's guide to Socratic questioning.* Lanham, MD: Rowman & Littlefield.

Singpurwalla, R. (2006). Reasoning with the irrational. *Ancient Philosophy, 26*(2), 243–258.

United Nations Human Rights Special Procedures. (2019). *Special Rapporteur on contemporary forms of racism, racial discrimination, xenophobia and related intolerance.*

Vorobej, M. (2006). *A theory of argument.* Cambridge: Cambridge University Press.

Walker, P. (2024). No 10 condemns London Theatre for hosting Black Out Nights. *Guardian*, 29 February. https://www.theguardian.com/stage/2024/feb/29/no-10-condemns-london-theatre-for-hosting-black-out-nights.

Winings, K. (2019). *White fragility: Why it's so hard for White people to talk about racism.* Boston, MA: Beacon Press.

Zembylas, M. (2022). The affective and political complexities of White shame and shaming: Pedagogical implications for anti-racist education. *Studies in Philosophy and Education, 41*, 635–652.

11

Trauma-informed approaches

Sam McNally

Introduction

We view the world through a lens coloured by our lived experience. The habits that we create to survive through adversity no longer serve us when it is time to thrive, and those existing in survival mode may be hypervigilant and alert to perceived threat even when requests made of them may seem perfectly reasonable to the other party. This chapter will explore the communication challenges for professionals supporting trauma-affected populations and consider the impact of trauma and its potential to distort messages and disrupt the flow of information. It will present the potential benefits of using approaches that are 'trauma-informed' (Harris & Fallot, 2001) to maximise the efficacy of communications.

Why trauma-informed approaches are important

Our nervous systems are wired by our prior experience in a way that is unique to each of us and goes some way towards determining our coping susceptibility to be stress-resilient or stress-vulnerable (Ebner & Singewald, 2017). The greatest challenges are that it is not always easy to identify an individual who is a trauma survivor, and that we, as helping professionals, may underestimate the long-term impact of trauma on a person's psychological and physiological health. In order to understand someone's experience, professionals often ask them to recount their past events, and this re-visiting of difficult, or in some cases intolerable, material has the potential to further re-traumatise the person, exacerbating the problems faced. Traditionally understood ways of working risk causing additional harm by implementing practices with characteristics that mirror past trauma. Approaches that are trauma-informed are grounded in an understanding of the pervasive biological, social, and psychological impacts of trauma exposure (Office for Health

DOI: 10.4324/9781003433248-14

Improvement & Disparities, 2022) and the benefits of supporting the whole individual rather than focusing on specific behaviours or presenting symptoms. The concept of trauma-informed approaches was introduced by Harris and Fallot (2001) when considering the most effective ways of providing services to populations who may have lost their sense of control and autonomy through being survivors of significant past trauma.

Complex trauma

For those with a history of complex trauma, it may be that conversations that we wouldn't traditionally think of as *difficult* are in fact overwhelming due to *stress susceptibility*. Each individual will differ in their perception to adverse stimuli; this can be affected by neurobiological mechanisms in childhood (Ebner & Singewald, 2017). It can be helpful to identify factors in an interaction in the here and now that may share stressors which bear similarity to the original trauma and cause a person to respond in a way that seems incongruent or excessive in the current circumstances. Even when significant lengths of time have elapsed since the trauma occurred, triggering factors such as language patterns, smells, or other environmental similarities can thrust people back into the time when they experienced the original trauma, causing them to respond to the original interaction rather than the current exchange.

The human body's response to complex childhood trauma causes adaptations to the brain at points of key development (Perry et al., 1995). When faced with a situation that we perceive as dangerous, it is a normal physiological response for the body to release cortisol and adrenaline (stress hormones) in preparation for a need to react to the threat. After the risk has diminished, and our sense that the perceived danger has dissipated, the body eliminates the stress hormones and returns to its previous neutral state. However, for those with neurobiological changes associated with their early trauma, they may find that their body remains stuck in this state of high alert, primed to respond to a hostile world filled with danger, and with a limbic system flooded with stress hormones which are chronically activated and causing an overreaction to perceived threat. Scientists have identified how these brain adaptations during early childhood development can lead to changes in reward and memory systems in the brains of these children (Perry et al., 1995). This can result in the person struggling to understand or interpret social cues and misreading facial expressions as being threatening or hostile, leading to them avoiding social interactions to prevent the onset of this toxic stress.

Trauma-informed conversation

The link between complex childhood trauma and later difficulties with perceiving threat is known as *latent vulnerability* (McCrory, 2020). Latent vulnerability puts a child or young person at greater risk than may be immediately obvious to helping professionals, as it makes it harder for the young person to build and maintain normal relationships. Although toxic stress and latent vulnerability are concerning, it isn't all bad news. The brain is also able to adapt to positive change, and the negative impact of brain adaptation to survive adversity in early childhood can be reversed with positive experiences as the brain continues to mature into adulthood. For this reason, conversations with helping professionals that recognise the impact of past trauma and help to guide young people onto a more resilient path are crucial for supporting social competency and helping to expand their window of tolerance (Siegel, 1999).

Relationships are everything

Research indicates that 85% of people facing multiple disadvantages in adulthood have previously experienced childhood trauma (Bramley & Fitzpatrick, 2015). Commentators in this field highlight the importance of positive relationships and safe environments to promote positive change (Bath, 2008; Sweeney et al., 2018). When we are tasked with the role of supporting children and young people burdened by a trauma history, evidence suggests that relationships are key (Substance Abuse and Mental Health Services Administration, 2014). Safe relationships are those grounded in connection and consistency. Human connection can be defined as affording people the opportunity to feel seen, heard, and valued (Brown, 2012). We are innately programmed for connection, and for children beginning to navigate the world and manage their emotions, this is far easier to achieve with a supportive adult with whom they can co-regulate big emotions (Naish et al., 2023). To communicate effectively with trauma-affected young people, it is important to remain mindful that interactions are likely to be impacted by past traumatic experience. Many survivors of trauma find absorbing verbal information challenging. This can be owing to hypervigilance around perceived safety and a hyperawareness of environmental factors which can be distracting during an interaction, but it can also be related to reduced concentration and loss of focus due to dissociation as a self-protection mechanism in times of high anxiety. For professionals unaware of the person's history, this may be perceived as disinterest or an unwillingness to engage. It can take time for trusting relationships to be forged, but people who have been hurt in a relationship can only be healed in a relationship (De Thierry, 2017), so professionals committed to investing time and effort to achieve meaningful interactions and empathic communication are key to recovery.

Trauma-informed conversations in education

Engagement within the education system is often the first significant source of interaction that a young person experiences beyond their familial relationships. Communication in schools is key. For children to learn, teachers must bridge the gap between their knowledge and the pupils' understanding to achieve instructional clarity. In addition to this, there should be a feedback loop where pupils seek clarification, ask questions, and give feedback (Engelbrecht-Alworth, 2023). However, it can be hard for pupils who are hypervigilant of their safety to be emotionally available to learn. One of the things that we seek to achieve in educational settings is to promote children's independence, but before we can effectively promote independence, the children must first have learned to rely on adults to maintain their safety and provide boundaries that are predictable.

Communication needs to begin with allowing the young person to explain their trauma triggers and working collaboratively to identify how best to help them feel safe. It is important that professionals avoid judgement and avoid interrupting young learners who have felt able to share this dialogue. There is a notable power imbalance between teacher and pupil, and this is most effectively addressed by setting clear and consistent boundaries that are respectful to both parties. The role of the professional is to facilitate the shift in communication from disconnection to reconnection. Effective communication can reduce isolation and reduce the risk of re-traumatisation. We can help young people to identify the *glimmers* – the positive elements in life which might be considered the opposite of triggers. Glimmers are small moments that may spark joy or happiness and act as cues to the nervous system that the person is safe. We can use these as building blocks to allow hope to flourish out of the darkness. It can feel incredibly empowering for the young person to take control of their triggers by counteracting these with the hope that is found in *glimmers*. Brown (2021) says the following of what is understood by connection: 'The energy that exists between people when they feel seen, heard, and valued; when they can give and receive without judgement; and when they derive sustenance and strength from the relationship' (Brown, 2021: 169).

Trauma-informed practice is not concerned with fixing or rescuing; it is about safety, trust, choice, empowerment, and collaboration, using open lines of communication to facilitate reconnection and to build upon positivity and hope. It also operates on a principle of clear cultural consideration.

Of course, schools are not just places of learning; communication is central to building relationships and achieving key milestones in social development. However, we know that children carrying the burden of trauma may be at higher risk of future negative social experience such as bullying and exclusion by peers due to a phenomenon known as stress generation (McCrory, 2020).

Case study: Mabel and Mr Smith

Mabel seems distracted in class, looking out of the window and seemingly daydreaming. Mr Smith asks Mabel a question about the lesson content, but Mabel is unable to answer. She looks panicked and shrugs her shoulders. Mr Smith offers further information as he walks towards Mabel with a smile, to try to evoke an answer. Other pupils turn to Mabel looking expectantly for her response.

Mabel feels her cheeks prickling and Mr Smith notes her eyes tear up as they dart from side to side. Mabel stands and slams her chair into the desk behind. She stomps out of the classroom swiping resources off of a table and slamming the door behind her. Some of the pupils chorus 'owwww!' and there is giggling. Mr Smith tells the class to settle down.

Mabel's story

Mabel has grown up as a care-experienced young person. She finds it difficult to trust adults because in her past those whom she should have been able to rely upon to keep her safe failed to protect her. Mabel likes her teacher, Mr Smith, and she has made good progress in his class, but she misread his facial expression on this occasion. A smile which was intended as encouraging and warm was received as the face of someone smirking at her and mocking her inability to answer the question she had been asked. That innocent question was interpreted as an attack, as Mabel's past trauma has left her stress-vulnerable and trapped within a narrow window of tolerance (Siegel, 1999). Mabel might also have a negative internal working model, causing a poor perception of self-worth based on her past relationships and experience of rejection (Naish et al., 2023).

Response to the case study: Mabel and Mr Smith

Mr Smith settles the class with a focused task and steps outside to speak with Mabel.

'I wonder if my asking you a question in front of the class felt overwhelming? I wonder if you were worried to answer in case you did not have the correct answer?'. By tentatively wondering about Mabel's emotional response, Mr Smith opens the line of communication for Mabel to explain her reaction. He does not assume to know how Mabel feels, but this empathic enquiry allows Mabel to have a voice.

Whilst Mabel explains her reaction, Mr Smith employs active listening skills: nodding and affirming, with appropriate, but not overbearing, eye contact, and without interrupting her. He stands next to Mabel but at a comfortable distance, respecting her personal space. Mabel explains that she felt embarrassed and as though Mr Smith was smirking at her. Mr Smith acknowledges that it must have been horrible to feel that she was being mocked, especially in front of her peers, and explains that he would never want Mabel to feel that way. He wonders out loud with Mabel how that situation may have played out differently.

Mr Smith recognises that Mabel's past experiences mean that she cannot always accurately read facial expressions and social cues, and this sometimes leads to defensive responses as a self-protection mechanism. He also realises that asking Mabel questions in front of the whole class without prior warning can also cause a flooding of stress hormones owing to her latent vulnerability. They agree a plan for next lesson where Mr Smith will write questions on the board and Mabel will put up her hand for the question she feels most comfortable to answer. This allows her to exercise some control, but also demonstrates to Mr Smith that Mabel is engaging in lessons and willing to contribute. This constitutes a mutually respectful arrangement which is trauma-informed.

Mabel needs a space where it is safe to make mistakes. She needs empathic commentary to coach her through experiences where she feels she has failed or may be rejected by her peers or teaching staff. This may involve helping Mabel to recognise and name her emotions, and providing responses that validate Mabel and give her a voice in situations when she feels disempowered.

Health

Hospitals and healthcare settings can be places synonymous with healing and recovery, but for some they may also be the source of trauma. Trauma-affected persons accessing healthcare may carry unrelated trauma histories or specific experience of medical trauma, both of which may affect their experience of healthcare services and the associated interactions with healthcare professionals. One reoccurring theme with those reporting medical trauma centres around faulty or ineffective communication. Research suggests that patients with a history of trauma report greater levels of negative interactions with healthcare professionals (Green et al., 2012). Green et al. (2015) have undertaken research using trauma-informed communication training with healthcare professionals to establish if these skills could be used to improve communication with patients who are trauma survivors. In line with a trauma-informed model, efforts were also made to ensure that the effects of trauma on the helping professionals were mitigated to prevent vicarious and secondary trauma. The training used the Risking Connection® (Sidran Institute, 2004) RICH© relationships model, which is embodied by Respect, Information, Connection, and Hope. Giller et al. (2005) assert that these factors are key in healing from trauma. One of the central features of this approach is that healthcare professionals are trained to assume that trauma survivors are present in every setting, and explicit acknowledgement of this is encouraged. There is no request or expectation that patients should make a disclosure of their history, but instead the potential stigma is addressed by being transparent about the known prevalence of trauma in all populations (Giller et al., 2005). This aligns with the tenets of trauma-informed approaches in mitigating re-traumatisation.

This chapter has explored how positive relationships can be restorative and reparative for trauma survivors. Positive relationship experiences are recalled more readily than negative recall of adversity owing to the way that attachment is represented in the mind (Holmes & Slade, 2018), leaving optimistic scope for healing trauma through forging empathic professional relationships, shaped with therapeutic conversations. These can be structured using the conversational concepts developed by linguistic philosopher Paul Grice, which were identified during analysis of effective conversational styles and became known as the 'Gricean maxims' (Grice, 1975, cited in Holmes & Slade, 2018). The purpose of these foundational concepts was to facilitate rational, coherent, and cooperative conversations. The maxims consist of four directions:

- Be truthful and have evidence for what you say (maxim of quality)
- Be succinct yet complete (maxim of quantity)
- Be relevant (relational maxim)
- Be clear and orderly (maxim of manner)

(Holmes & Slade, 2018: 88)

By using these four concepts to shape interactions, the helping professional can begin to develop trust and transparency.

Case study: Oliver and the medical team

Oliver has been admitted to hospital after a road traffic collision. Oliver requires surgery but is reluctant to consent after his father died following an unexpected cardiac arrest during a routine operation at another hospital four years prior.

Oliver presents as highly anxious and is keen to self-discharge, but the medical team are very concerned that without surgical intervention, Oliver may lose his hand. The surgeon and the anaesthetist have tried without success to explain the benefits and risks of the surgery to Oliver.

Oliver is calmer and more responsive with one of the nursing associates in the Emergency Ward. Layla has been able to identify Oliver's concerns and has explained the situation regarding Oliver's father to the surgical team. Layla has been tasked with trying to convince Oliver that he really does need to undergo the surgery to his hand.

There are various factors in this case which may impact the communication between Oliver and the helping professionals. Oliver is currently experiencing significant pain, fear, and anxiety, which will all impact his ability to receive information and make informed decisions regarding his care. He is also hugely focused on the surgery four years ago which resulted in the unexpected death of his father.

Oliver appears to have started to build a trusting relationship with Layla from the nursing team and has already made honest disclosures regarding his prior experience and associated fear.

The surgical team have failed to gain consent from Oliver to go to theatre, so Layla needs to try to effectively communicate the reasons for undergoing the surgery to Oliver in order that he is able to give or withhold informed consent.

In hospital settings it may be that some members of the multidisciplinary team (MDT) are best placed to open the dialogue around difficult conversations because they have built a rapport with the patient, or perhaps because they have more time available to listen to the patient and hear their concerns in an unrushed manner. In this case, for example, it is likely that the patient will then also need to be seen by the medics to confirm consent, but the foundations for this interaction may have been laid in the previous conversation with members of the wider MDT such as Layla. This factor will be crucial in ensuring a warm and empathic dyad within which the dialogue can be explored, allowing Oliver to have his concerns heard and offering the emotional safety of a familiar face.

Response to the Case study: Oliver and the medical team

Layla takes the time to sit with Oliver and listen to his experience of his father dying whilst under general anaesthetic. She uses active listening and empathically responds, acknowledging how difficult it must have been and how hard it must be now – being in hospital after experiencing loss in a similar setting.

Layla tells Oliver that there are risks with any surgery, but owing to his uncomplicated medical history, the risks are low. She offers the numbers of comparable, successful surgeries that have been performed at the NHS Trust in the previous three years (quantity maxim).

She explains the steps of the anaesthetic process (as this is Oliver's major concern) and advises that the anaesthetist will be happy to explain the medical process in detail (maxim of quality). She reassures Oliver that it is understandable that he is anxious, and confirms that she will stay with him whilst he speaks to the anaesthetist if that is his preference.

Oliver begins to catastrophise about unrelated medical concerns. Layla brings the conversation calmly and sensitively back to the key elements and risk factors for the procedure and reminds him of the positives of the surgery (relational maxim).

Finally, she helps Oliver to summarise his key concerns so that he feels empowered to ask the surgeon for reassurance regarding these specific elements (maxim of manner). She offers to advocate using the list of concerns if Oliver becomes overwhelmed during the discussion with the surgeon. With Layla's support, Oliver feels he fully understands the risks and is able to provide his informed consent to go ahead with the surgery.

Once the patient is feeling secure to engage in open dialogue, the focus shifts to the language used and the structure of the conversation. In addition to avoiding interruptions to the flow of dialogue, it is important to really listen to achieve understanding of the patients' perspective. Covey famously observed how 'most people do not listen with the intent to understand; they listen with the intent to reply' (Covey, 1989: 239), which negatively impacts the ability to gain insight inside another person's frame of reference. It is important to truly receive their communication in order to obtain accurate data and to avoid projecting our own interpretation. It can also be incredibly cathartic for a person to share their narrative with an interested other. It validates their experience, which can help to remove associated shame.

Social care

Populations engaging with the social care system are especially likely to have experienced trauma. Many of the service users that helping professionals support will present with maladaptive coping mechanisms and a view of the world that is shaped by their history of trauma. Trauma-informed practices and approaches can be useful in strengthening a therapeutic alliance and in facilitating post-traumatic growth (Levenson, 2017). When professionals encounter service-users who are challenging, aggressive, or seemingly obstructive, it can be easy to find ourselves frustrated and asking, 'what is wrong with them?', but trauma-informed practice requires a shift in that thinking towards instead wondering 'what happened to them?' Once we move to the more accepting and less judgemental position of exploring the root causes of the presenting behaviours, which are too often indicators of trauma and interrelated emotional wounds, professionals can be part of the process of interrupting the intergenerational cycle of victimisation (Harris & Fallot, 2001).

Case study: Brooke's engagement with children's services

Brooke has struggled with alcohol dependency since adolescence. She now has a 4-year-old son, Wesley, who is subject to a Child in Need Plan (CiN, The Children Act, 1989: S17). Brooke wants to do her best for Wesley, but sometimes she becomes overwhelmed and in times of high stress she tends to use alcohol to numb the pain associated with poverty and loneliness. Wesley's father is serving a custodial sentence for violent crime and has had no contact since Wesley turned a year. He was violent towards Brooke before and during her pregnancy and she reports being glad that contact has ceased.

Brooke has been advised by her social worker, Joe, that she needs to attend a drug and alcohol addiction group to demonstrate her commitment to abstaining from alcohol use when Wesley is in her care. She is angry because she feels that Joe is saying she is a bad mother and is worried that if the group leaders undertake routine drug and alcohol testing this may result in Wesley being removed from her care.

Brooke feels as though the request for her to attend the addiction group is a punishment. She feels as though Joe is waiting for her to slip up and that this will provide a reason to remove Wesley from her care. Brooke's early developmental environment demanded a relational strategy of independence. She was unable to rely on adults to meet her needs or maintain her safety, so she quickly became self-sufficient and rejected any attempts to help her, instead trusting only herself to be relied upon. Her lack of a secure attachment figure in childhood has impacted her approach to parenting her own son. Brooke's internal working model has been adapted by her insecure attachments in early childhood, meaning that her responses to perceived threats from others are faulty. Joe's attempts to put a support network in place and assist Brooke in breaking free of her alcohol addiction have been received as an attack, and her learned inflexibility makes her resistant to change and suspicious of help. Brooke experiences crippling shame and punishes herself far more harshly with self-expectation than in respect of the standards she holds for others. Shame can be indicative of shifts in cognitive schemata where a person's worldview is impacted by prior experience (Iqbal, 2015). Survivors of trauma may find that they develop their understanding of the world by organising their past experiences and aligning these to assimilate new knowledge into their pre-existing schemata. This distorted worldview impacts relationships by causing the person to potentially overestimate risk owing to their contaminated memory from past experience. In Brooke's case she is aware that professionals have thought poorly of her in the past, especially in relation to her alcohol use. Therefore, her assumption is that Joe's opinion of her is negative. Joe can address this by allowing Brooke the time and safe space to share her experience and by affording her the opportunity to be heard. 'Shame dies when stories are told in safe places' (Voskamp, 2016), so listening is vital.

Another element that is important to consider here is the impact that these interactions have on the helping professionals. One of the key tenets of trauma-informed practice is recognising that the helping professional can also be vicariously affected by trauma of the client, pupil, or patient. This can be mitigated by employing supportive supervision for professionals working closely with trauma-affected populations. The difficult conversation between Brooke and Joe should be viewed as having the potential to negatively impact the well-being and esteem of both parties. Research suggests that trauma-informed supervision may be key in managing the pervasive impact of trauma in both clients and helping professionals (McNally, 2022).

Response to the case study: Brooke's engagement with children's services

Joe listens to Brooke as she explains her past experience and has empathy around why she feels that alcohol can numb the pain associated with difficult experience. Joe employs active listening and does not interrupt Brooke, despite disagreeing with the position she holds on some matters. Brooke tells Joe that she has never previously felt that professionals had listened to her story; instead they always seem quick to 'take the moral high ground' and want to 'fix her'. Joe recognises that he needs to empower Brooke to want to make the changes she needs to make herself rather than through fear of having Wesley removed from her care. He makes sure that, although perhaps not the exact path Brooke may have chosen, she still maintains control over some choices related to her treatment and recovery.

Joe also takes the case back to clinical supervision. As well as his supervisor helping him to formulate the most effective ways to support Brooke's recovery, he allows Joe the opportunity to reflect on his own emotional response to the history that Brooke has shared and consider the burden of hearing this detail of violent domestic abuse. Joe considers how he can use his empathic response to motivate him to keep supporting Brooke even when her recovery faulters. He also takes the advice of his supervisor to ensure he prioritises self-care, remembering that trauma can be contagious. He discusses transference with his supervisor and holds in mind that when Brooke directs her anger and blame at Joe, this is often a response to toxic relationships from her past where people have hurt her or let her down. Joe tries to remember that the negativity that is directed his way may just be Brooke's contaminated cognitive schemata affecting how she receives communication in the here and now.

Conclusion

Trauma-informed processes are universally positive for all, and vital for those carrying the burden of trauma in all of these contexts. Communication, and especially difficult conversations, may be particularly challenging for populations whose receptive language skills are impacted by difficulty in understanding facial expressions and gestures. For helping professionals, it can be easy to misread dissociation and hypervigilance as disinterest or overreaction and to fail to recognise that responses are fuelled by negative past experiences rather than being disproportionate or incongruent responses to innocuous requests in the here and now. By communicating using methods that are trauma-informed, both parties are protected from harm and conscious routes towards healing are forged.

Key takeaways

- Professionals will not always know about a client, pupil, or service-user's past trauma. A universal approach that follows trauma-informed principles is therefore good for all, and essential for many
- Ensure communication is clear and respectful. Recognise that the burden of trauma can impact the way that communication is received and perceived. Trauma-informed approaches allow processes that achieve equity
- All communication relating to the individual should be framed to ask *not* 'what is wrong with them?' but rather 'what happened to them?' This allows professionals to consider the possibility of mis-matched responses in interactions
- Trauma responses differ in each individual. Try to provide an environment that feels physically and emotionally safe before engaging in communication. Use open body language and appropriate eye contact, but avoid physical touch without explicit consent, and respect personal space
- Let the client, pupil, or service-user speak, avoiding interruptions, judgement, and without trying to *fix* things. Remember: 'Shame dies when stories are told in safe places' (Voskamp, 2016).

References

Bath, H. (2008). The three pillars of trauma-informed care. *Reclaiming Children and Youth, 1*(3), 17–21.

Bramley G., & Fitzpatrick, S. (2015). Hard edges: Mapping severe and multiple disadvantage – England. Lankelly Chase Foundation.

Brown, B. (2012). *Daring greatly: How the courage to be vulnerable transforms the way we live, love, parent and lead*. New York: Gotham.

Brown, B. (2021). *Atlas of the heart: Mapping meaningful connection and the language of human experience*. London: Vermilion.

The Children Act. (1989). Child in Need Plan (CiN). The Children Act 1989, Section 17. https://www.legislation.gov.uk/ukpga/1989/41/section/17.

Covey, S. (1989). *The seven habits of highly effective people.* London: Simon & Schuster UK.

De Thierry, B. (2017). *The simple guide to child trauma.* London: Jessica Kingsley Publishers.

Ebner, K., & Singewald, N. (2017). Individual differences in stress susceptibility and stress inhibitory mechanisms. *Current Opinion in Behavioural Sciences, 14,* 54–64.

Engelbrecht-Alworth, E. (2023). The Main Functions of Communication in a Well-Functioning School.

Giller, E., Vermilyea, E., & Steele, T. (2005). Risking connection: Helping agencies embrace relational work with trauma survivors. https://traumaticstressinstitute. org/wp-content/uploads/2012/05/Risking-Connection-Helping-Agencies-Embrace-Relational-Work-with-Trauma-Survivors1.pdf.

Green, B., Kaltman, S., Chung, J., Holt, M., Jackson, S., & Dozier, M. (2012). Attachment and healthcare relationships in low-income women with trauma histories: A qualitative study. *Journal of Trauma & Dissociation, 13*(2), 190–208.

Green B., Saunders, P., Power, E., Dass-Brailsford, P., Mete, M., & Giller E. (2015). Trauma-informed medical care: A CME communication training for primary care providers. *Family Medicine, 47*(1), 7–14.

Harris M., & Fallot R. (Eds.). (2001). *Using trauma theory to design service systems, 89* (pp. 33–46). San Francisco, CA: Jossey-Bass.

Holmes, J., & Slade, A. (2018). *Attachment in Therapeutic Practice.* Thousand Oaks, CA: Sage.

Iqbal, A. (2015). The ethical considerations of counselling psychologists working with trauma: Is there a risk of vicarious traumatisation? *Counselling Psychology Review, 30,* 44–51.

Levenson, J. (2017). Trauma-informed social work practice. *Social Work, 62*(2), 105–113.

McCrory, E. (2020). *Childhood adversity and the brain: What have we learnt?* https://www.eif.org.uk/blog/childhood-adversity-and-the-brain-what-have-we-learnt.

McNally, S. (2022). Using hermeneutic phenomenology and visual representation to explore trauma in the primary classroom: The case for classroom teachers to access supervision. https://pure.port.ac.uk/ws/portalfiles/portal/76147073/ S.McNally_UP641888_with_MA2.pdf.

Naish, S., Oakley, A., O'Brien, H., Penna, S., & Thrower, D. (2023). *The A–Z of trauma-informed teaching.* London: Jessica Kingsley Publishers.

Office for Health Improvement & Disparities. (2022). *Guidance: Working definition of trauma-informed practice.* https://www.gov.uk/government/publications/ working-definition-of-trauma-informed-practice/working-definition-of-trauma-informed-practice.

Perry, B., Pollard, R., Blakley, T., Baker, W., & Viglante, D. (1995). Childhood trauma, the neurobiology of adaptation, and 'use-dependent' development of the brain: How states become traits. *Infant Mental Health Journal, 16*(4), 271–291.

Sidran Institute. (2004). Risking Connection® Trainee outcome research: A pilot study. https://traumaticstressinstitute.org/wp-content/uploads/2012/05/RC-Trainee-Outcome-Pilot-Study.pdf.

Siegel, D. (1999). *The developing mind*. New York: Guildford Press.

Substance Abuse and Mental Health Services Administration. (2014). *SAMHSA's concept of trauma and guidance for a trauma-informed approach*. Rockville, MD: Substance Abuse and Mental Health Services Administration.

Sweeney, A., Filson, B., Kennedy, A., Collinson, L., & Gillard, S. (2018). A paradigm shift: Relationships in trauma-informed mental health services. *The British Journal of Psychiatry*, *24*(5), 319–333.

Voskamp, A. (2016). Author quote on X. https://x.com/AnnVoskamp/status/78294 1512061575168.

12

Conclusion

As we stated in our introduction, we hope that the ideas and concepts discussed in this book provide you with the tools you need to approach difficult conversations with less trepidation. Whatever our profession, as humans we will all, at some point in our personal or professional lives, be forced to have conversations that we would rather not have. As discussed in many of the chapters, our brain interprets these conversations as a threat and tries with all its might to persuade us to run away or hide. It takes courage, integrity, and stamina to resist this fight, flight, freeze response. We hope that, in these situations, you can find something in our book that will help.

The topics in the final section: Talking About What Really Matters are based on the personal experiences of the authors and, as such, provide an opportunity for us all to develop a more empathetic understanding of current issues.

As social beings, conversations are at the very heart of what makes us human. They bring us a sense of shared happiness, a feeling of belonging, a belief that we matter to others, but at their most difficult, they can also cause us to feel ashamed, angry, or hurt and lead to polarisation and permanent rifts. But this is all avoidable if we understand why we respond the way we do and why others respond the way they do. We hope, if nothing else, that what we discuss in this book gives pause for thought and provides you with strategies that can prevent difficult conversations from spiralling into disagreements or irreconcilable arguments.

As professionals in education, health and social care, we must be aware of our perceived power in any conversation with students, patients, or service-users. Conversations have little to do with the words we use and a great deal to do with the messages we give. If difficult conversations are to be

 DOI: 10.4324/9781003433248-15

successful, we must be as aware of our body language, gestures, and the implied intent behind the language we use.

Difficult conversations are multifaceted, often complicated, and almost always emotionally exhausting. But if you listen effectively, respond with genuineness and understand why and how it can all go wrong, there is always the chance that, like a superhero, you can save the day. With the right skills, knowledge, and experience, it is possible to move a conversation from challenging to effective, from problematic to solution-focused, from polarised to collaborative.

Throughout our book we have tried to emphasise that it is not what the conversation is about that matters, but about why we are having it. Conversations are not about who is right or who is wrong; they are about how we can move forward together – and that can only happen if we work hard to understand each other's story and the emotions that underpin what is being communicated to us. Whether we are talking about race or gender or trauma, whether we are talking with children or adolescents or adults, if a conversation is to be successful, everyone involved must understand that their voice matters.

Like everything in life, including giving up crisps and chocolate, these things are easy to say and hard to do. But when we manage it, when we successfully navigate a difficult conversation, when something that seemed impossible becomes possible or we find a solution to a seemingly insolvable problem, the sense of achievement makes it all worthwhile.

As with most things in life, there is no 'one-size-fits-all' solution; every conversation is unique, every situation is different. But we hope that this book gives you the confidence to try, so that instead of dreading difficult conversations you can see them as opportunities. As is clear from the experiences of Rylee, Mia, and Sam in the final part, conversations about race, trauma, and gender can be particularly challenging, but the most difficult conversations are also the most worthwhile. A difficult conversation can become a catalyst for change.

Without everyday conversations, we are lonely; without difficult conversations, we are stuck.

Writing a book is always a journey, and like most journeys it never really finishes. There is always more to say, more to discover, more to learn. That is also true of conversations. But reflecting on the difficult conversations we have had in the past, talking to others about the difficult conversations they have had, and remembering how it felt when it all went wrong, has made us realise how much we can all learn from each other.

We hope this book gives you the courage to speak up when it is the right thing to do, the patience to listen when time is at a premium, and the skills to make every difficult conversation a conversation that really matters.

Index

Note: **Bold** page numbers refer to tables.

For Product Safety Concerns and Information please contact our EU
representative GPSR@taylorandfrancis.com
Taylor & Francis Verlag GmbH, Kaufingerstraße 24, 80331 München, Germany

www.ingramcontent.com/pod-product-compliance
Lightning Source LLC
Chambersburg PA
CBHW070338270326
41926CB00017B/3906